The Postmodern Controversy

The Postmodern Controversy

Understanding Richard Rorty, Jacques Derrida and Jürgen Habermas

Prasenjit Biswas

RAWAT PUBLICATIONS
Jaipur • New Delhi • Bangalore • Guwahati • Kolkata

ISBN 978-81-7033-861-1

Reprinted, 2021

Published by
Prem Rawat for **Rawat Publications**
Satyam Apts, Sector 3, Jawahar Nagar, Jaipur 302 004 (India)
Phones: 0141 265 1748 / 265 7006
E-mail: info@rawatbooks.com
Website: www.rawatbooks.com

New Delhi Office
4858/24, Ansari Road, Daryaganj, New Delhi 110 002
Phone: 011 2326 3290

Also at *Bangalore, Guwahati* and *Kolkata*

Typeset by Rawat Computers, Jaipur
Printed and bound in India

Dedicated to

My Parents

Purnima Biswas and Gopendranath Biswas

Contents

Acknowledgements

I have had an immensely rich, profound and precious experience of intellectual sagacity in discussing intricate philosophical issues pertaining to this work with Professor M.M. Agrawal. With his Socratic temperament, he not only listened to my polemics, but always showed me a 'resting place', a place of difference and responsibility.

I record here my gratitude to colleagues like Professors Milind Malshe, A. Ramanathan, P.R. Bhat, K. Subuddhi, V.C.Thomas and Bijoy H.Boruah for bringing me rich insights of Philosophy, catalysed by friends like Indrani, Rakesh and Nirmal and students like Upendra and Rafi and Ravi. I also thank my teacher, Dr S.C. Daniel, for his kind help and encouragement throughout half a decade of writing this book. My friends, Chandanda and Sushy Boudi, bind me in their eternal debt by their immense sacrifices for me.

I acknowledge the profound intellectual influence of Professor Mrinal Miri, which came through listening to and interacting with him.

I carry with me the flickers of Derridean insight generated in me by Gayatri Chakraborty Spivak, who most kindly consented to discuss Derrida with me.

I express my gratitude to Professor Goutam Biswas, Nikunja Biswas, Bijoy Mukherjee and Asha Mukherjee for sustaining my interest in philosophising for the last six years through their discourses with me. I express my gratitude to Professor Daya Krishna and Professor Suresh Chandra for their critical questioning of the concepts and arguments through which I progressed.

I owe a great debt to the American studies Research Centre, Hyderabad, for providing me two teacher study grants to finish my works on Richard Rorty and Jacques Derrida during March and September 1996.

I also record here my sincerest gratitude to the Jawaharlal Nehru Memorial Fund for offering me the Jawaharlal Nehru Scholarship, which funded my doctoral studies during 1997-98.

Finally, I have no words to express my debt to Debasish Choudhury, Rajesh, Sukalpa, Chittaranjan, Dr. Butola, Bhaskarjyoti and all other friends who have directly contributed to the production of this work in innumerable ways.

I record here my deepest gratitude to Ashok Acharya for mentoring me in Continental Philosophy. I also record here the loving indulgence of Udayonda and Tilottamadi in shaping some of my praxi-oriented ideas.

I also thank Professor Apurba K. Baruah and Monorama Sharma in their efforts to keep up an interventionist spirit in me.

Prasenjit Biswas

I

Introduction

The Sources of Postmodern Thought

The problematique of the critique of knowledge as developed by postmodern thinkers like Richard Rorty and Jacques Derrida on the one hand, and modern thinkers like Jurgen Habermas on the other, constitute the raging controversy that involves crucial epistemic concerns like truth and reason. Even though all three thinkers join in a critique of metaphysical foundations of knowledge as conceived within the 'modern' concept of knowledge, their mode of criticism is so different that they take varied routes and derive different conclusions. This creates a problem in appropriating them in a linear-homogeneous comparison and thereby turns it into a task of comparison of the mutually incommensurable positions taken by these three philosophers.

The postmodern debunking of 'truth' as a validating concept is based upon a methodological shift in the very idea of reality. Reality is no longer conceived to be a realm outside one's senses or concepts possessed by someone, rather it is conceived as an articulation by a human subject positioned/situated within an already construed frame of reference. So postmodern thought evolves a principle of 'situated knowledge' that truth or reason as a constitutive element and thereby abandons the objective, theory-independent and neutral notion of truth to be discovered by a kind of reason that is essentially uninfluenced by any prior epistemic commitments. This, however, does not mean that 'situated knowledge' enshrines a prior epistemic commitment on the part of the knower; rather, it merely looks into how the knower is situated within a frame of reference that manifests along any cognitive activity of the knower, be it claims of knowledge or belief. Given this shift from the idea of objectivity to 'situated knowledge', claims of knowledge no longer redeem any transcendental-subjective or objective focus; rather, it emanates from an interrogation of what goes into making a body of knowledge such as 'philosophy'.

Configuring 'Knowledge'

Philosophy is the space opened up by 'our access to the world', a space that 'explains' our 'knowledge' of the world. Philosophical knowledge is 'reflective' and 'reflexive' in character: It is reflective to the extent that it represents the world in the conceptual description that philosophy creates through reflection and it is reflexive to the extent that it comes back to the world with its conceptual description of the world. Therefore, philosophical knowledge turns knowledge both into a subject of reflection/representation as well as reflexion. Philosophical knowledge can be distinguished from knowledge of particulars by these special functions of reflection and reflexion because both these give knowledge an in-built power to account for knowledge of particulars. This becomes evident in the a priori modes of knowledge, when even without 'knowledge of particulars', knowledge of something can be attained. Therefore, knowledge which is able to reflect and reflex is philosophical in character and such philosophical knowledge can be called 'knowledge-as-such', which makes knowledge of something a subject of description and analysis.[1]

An account of philosophical knowledge or knowledge-as-such has three aspects: (1) the role of the human subject as the knower, (2) knowing 'about' the world, and (3) returning to the concrete with what is already known, that is, attainment of a capacity to have access to the world on the basis of what is 'known about'. All these three aspects empower the human subject to have a grasp of the world and make a claim about the world. Further, these three aspects are coordinated and performed in an efficient way if these basic roles and acts are 'theorised'. Such a theorisation will obviously incorporate the role of the human subject and her basic drives for knowledge. Theory is meant to first comprehend this whole process of knowledge and then to provide an interpretative/explanatory support for our claims of knowledge. Again, all these three aspects of knowledge-as-such are theorised in a theory of knowledge. The theorisation depends upon the introspection within knowledge-as-such about its own constitution, because such introspection is engendered not only in understanding the world, but also in assessing its own efficacy. This introspection within knowledge-as-such assumes self-reflexivity and thereby gives rise to a criterion of internal self-sufficiency, with which it reflects and reflexes upon the world.

1. This introspection within knowledge-as-such is meaningful in two ways primarily: by way of transparency and by way of confirmation. In the first, it provides a criterion to adjudge a theory by its own self-evaluative criterion and in the second, an external criterion is created to place a theory over and against the world that it describes.
2. The principle of reason is confirmed and based upon such internal and external criteria of transparency and confirmation. Reason as an exercise of the human faculty(ies), later known as 'mind', is given different descriptions by either distinguishing and separating the two criteria or by colluding it in a single theory.
3. The internal and external criteria of transparency and confirmation act as presuppositions of a theory of knowledge. In applying such a theory to cases of

knowledge and claims of knowledge, such criteria themselves and claims of knowledge are never the 'subject' of these cases and claims, rather the cases and claims are the 'subject' of these criteria.

4. One implication of this 'subjectification' of cases and claims of knowledge is that knowledge of something is always already a subject of judging whether it fulfils these criteria or not. This further implies that claims engendering out of knowledge situations require an internal and external justification. The task for a theory of knowledge is to provide that kind of justification by way of mapping claims and cases of knowledge within knowledge-as-such.
5. This justificatory move of knowledge of something within philosophical knowledge is self-critical, and directed to the attainment of truth-value, or the status of truth. Theory of knowledge employs self-critical moves to gain authenticity.

Critique of Knowledge

Critique of knowledge originates from an interrogation of the concept of knowledge as available within a theory of knowledge. The critique engages itself with the 'how' and 'what' of the concept of knowledge, which means that the 'concepts' with their 'limits' that go into making a concept of knowledge are analysed in a critique of knowledge. Therefore, one can say that critique of knowledge makes knowledge-as-such its subject of analysis by analysing the concept of knowledge embedded in it. Further, critique of knowledge locates an explanatory gap in a theory and re-orients it to overcome that limitation. Critique of knowledge, therefore, gives rise to a re-oriented theory of knowledge and hence gives rise to a 'new' theory of knowledge by way of modifying the shortcomings of an earlier theory of knowledge. In other words, themes within a theory of knowledge supply the cues for interrogation for a critique and the critique problematises these themes by locating an 'explanatory gap' in the theory itself and, finally, offers new solutions to the problems embedded in the earlier solution by enacting another interpretation/explanation, ultimately by giving another theory of knowledge.

1. In the case of the Cartesian critique of knowledge, the internal self-sufficiency of knowledge and the external confirmation of knowledge collapsed into a singular criterion of certitude of the ego-self known through meditations within one's mind. The external criterion of confirmation was subjected under the criterion of self-certitude giving rise to a bi-polarity between mind(self) and world, in which the mind can exclude the world by conceiving an idea of the world. The central thematic of Cartesian critique became an interrogation of the certitude of external reality and a surge for self-subsistent ideas within the mental realm that form knowledge.[2]
2. Hume[3] interrogated this Cartesian meditative process by pointing out that ideas do not have a basis, except in impressions of the world through our senses and such sense-data can only give rise to native realisation. Hume rejected both Cartesian claims that reason can comprehend the world and that external reality can be known in ideas. Reason, for Hume, could only give rise to belief about the external world and nothing more.
3. The Cartesian critique of knowledge producing scepticism about the world, later to be realised only in ideas and in the Humean radicalisation of Cartesian doubt, prevailed over Kant while asking the question, "What is the condition of possibility of experiencing the world?" (paraphrased by me). In discussing the condition of possibility, Kant thematised the human mind as the faculty of knowledge with its categories of understanding leaving aside the passive objects of knowledge in the world as 'phenomena' constituted by the 'representations' of thing-in-itself. Such a thematisation of the human mind domesticated the external world in terms of transcendentally deduced categories that subsume concepts under it, which further

subsumes representations. Therefore, the Kantian condition of possibility produces a theory of knowledge that presupposes the presence of human consciousness as 'representation in general', endowing the capacity to deduce categories and concepts to have a grasp of the world. This presupposes an active human consciousness in the act of uniting manifold representations within a unity of experience. The subject of this unity of experience is a singular 'I', which continues in a consciousness of the representation. Kant closes off his critique of any possibility of multiplicity of experiences of the same object by the same 'self' conditioning its experiences into a unity by being acted upon by a conscious self as a necessity. Kant locates the idea of the self as the centre of consciousness. Still, he does not explain its self-subsistent transparency. The relationship between consciousness and what it endows in the faculty of the human self is taken to be primitive and given.[4]

4. This givenness of consciousness persists in Hegel's speculative critique of Kant for his non-thematisation of the contradiction between consciousness as 'form' and its 'content', which is an object 'x', sublated in an identity within consciousness. This sublation takes place through abstraction which assumes the form of a contradiction to be dissolved in the 'being'. Hegel's critique of Kant goes in the Kantian direction of a theory of knowledge that makes knowledge the speculative reappropriation of being in human consciousness.[5]
5. The 'explanatory gap' in Kant's theory of knowledge is created by the givenness of consciousness as a general form of representation that does not explain its relationship with categorical knowledge. Husserl explains this relationship between consciousness and categorical knowledge by attributing the noesis ('meaning-giving act'), that is the directionality of consciousness onto the pure and ideal object extracted through eidetic reduction and/

or transcendental reduction, to consciousness itself. Participation of consciousness in the meaning-giving act is again by an enveloping of the world within transcendental ego and, hence, again a one-sided abstraction of/for the world.[6]

6. Heidegger radicalises this problem of consciousness in his project of overcoming metaphysics in so far as philosophy conceived the world as a world within consciousness. Heidegger's reinterpretation combined the question of knowing the world with the question of consciousness in a two-fold logic: one, knowledge of the world is knowledge of the being of the world and two, knowledge of the being of the world is knowledge of being in the world. He introduces the concept of being as something which is just there; the moment anything is known in the world, it is known by a being, it is being's knowledge of other beings. This knowledge is just a disclosure of other beings, the way they appear, but not the way they are. In such a disclosure, one is merely conscious of oneself as a being among other beings, knowing neither what there is, nor what constitutes the being in oneself. Therefore, there is a primordial absence of knowledge of being in being's knowledge, which is merely a consciousness of other beings in the way they are disclosed in one's consciousness. This primordial absence of knowledge shows that consciousness does not immediately have the capacity to know the world fully; it is limited to the extent to which the world is disclosed in one's consciousness. This could be considered as a critique of immanence of consciousness, which was hitherto treated as either a given (in Kant) or as a source of transcendental knowledge. It could also be considered as a critique of the condition of possibility of knowledge because it indicates a possibility of impossibility of knowledge.

As there is just a disclosure of the being of the world in the form of the being of the other in being's knowledge, which is also a disclosure of the being of the self in knowledge, knowledge can never be complete and unitary, but always fractured between the being of the other and the being of the self. This chasm within being's knowledge reveals being as aporetic in being's knowledge, which it recognises to be knowledge of the self and the other as well. Heidegger sees this state of knowledge as forgetfulness of being, which is forgetting of the being of all beings. The forgetfulness appears in its current form due to exaggeration of being's knowledge as authentic and complete. Therefore, Heidegger prescribed a method of 'destruction' of knowledge, which identified being's knowledge as drawing an identity between being and claimed knowledge of being in various human sciences. This destruction is directed at knowledge claimed to be knowledge of being as claimed by beings. It is directed in this way to reveal the ignorance of being about being to itself, so that being searches out its authentic face with an authentic understanding of being. It is interesting to note here that destruction reveals that being's knowledge of the world is incomplete and this incompleteness is revealed from being's knowledge itself. This is how destruction belongs to construction of that incomplete knowledge by the being and hence falls within the same logic of construction, which can never know the being. At the level of destruction, being of the incomplete knowledge is revealed in the form of beings who know it and from this the being can only be further distant. Therefore, destruction is a method of knowing the being, it is concealed as soon as knowledge of being as being's knowledge of itself and others are disclosed. Knowledge of being remains perpetually concealed in being's knowledge. This shows that the attempt of knowing or having knowledge of the world is never complete as it is constituted by the very possibility of impossibility of knowledge. This is what Heidegger calls 'being' under erasure and designates it with a 'cross' in the world. Being in this form as a possibility of impossibility simply means the impossibility of full and total realisation of being by being in the existential and temporal conditions of its possibility, i.e., the possibility of being. The absolute impossibility is its ultimate possibility and this is how being is to be realised by beings. Only when the absolute impossibility of being takes over the possibility of being is there death, the most authentic moment of being, which makes possible a simultaneous possibility and impossibility of being.[7]

'Problems' in the Critique of Knowledge

The whole terrain of critique of knowledge is a movement from self-certain construction of knowledge to what makes such knowledge possible. Within this terrain, the critique turns introspective to check whether the theory of knowledge that explains knowledge has internal consistency and external confirmation, but that merely closes it to a certain authoritative claim of knowledge. It utilises the concepts available within the theory for the ratification of the theory, but an interrogation of those concepts from within and without remains open. From within, the relationship of knowledge-as-such with the given is a source of explanatory gap, retaining which the theory of knowledge fulfils its purpose. From without, the claim of confirmation of knowledge appears problematic once the claim is placed against the realm of objects.[8] A critique of knowledge, therefore, brings a consistency within theory by utilising the internal tools, which it opens up to an external realm of objects lying beyond. A Cartesian-Kantian-Husserlian critique manages to bypass this external realm by closing a theory upon objects appropriated within it. The Heideggerian critique demonstrates that an appropriation of being in knowledge is possible only by abandoning the claim of completeness of knowledge and being remains not only as surplus over knowledge, but also as an external.

Therefore, certain problems could be located within a critique of knowledge. Phenomenality of the phenomenon can only be described within a theory of which a critique is possible on the 'condition' that the knowledge of the phenomenon does not include the perspective from which it is known. Kantian-Husserlian prioritisation of the consciousness leads to knowing how consciousness takes a grasp of the world without knowing what the consciousness is. This only shows that knowledge-as-such is compared on the negative condition that the critique cannot subject consciousness to its analytical focus. This may re-establish that both the theory and its critique are subjects of the negative condition that consciousness can't be brought under their purview. What happens in this kind of a situation is that (1) knowledge-as-such is constituted by a metaphysical subsumption/sublation of the world under consciousness and (2) there is a phenomenological reduction of the world under consciousness. In both these cases, the question of theorising knowledge-as-such derives its epistemic explanation from the metaphysical or the phenomenological prioritisation of human consciousness, which does not allow knowledge an independent roadmap to confirm itself in the world by implying only a guided access to the world. The negative condition that knowledge-as-such must exclude the realm of the objects by just taking the representation within human beings in the contact of a knowledge-situation lies in terms of situating being in the world. Situating being in the world as belonging to both being and 'being of beings' shows that it belongs to neither of them, as being of beings and being cannot exist both ways.[9] This peculiarity of situation of the human being as a being among beings and as a being of the beings demonstrates the negative condition of exclusion of one mode from another. This peculiarity of human beings is expressed in knowledge and specially in philosophical knowledge, embodying theories and their critique. It implies that human knowledge is merely situational and contextual and being as the ultimate ground of human knowledge is only partially retrieved, rather it is put under 'erasure' in knowledge situations. Therefore, being as the being of all beings is an ontology that makes human knowledge subject to its ontos without even allowing its realisation within the limits of knowledge. So this question of knowledge becomes the question of being, which only partially reveals the being of what is in the form of knowledge.

Distinction between Postmodern and Modern Critique of Knowledge

We read in the previous discussion a clear distinction of styles of critiques. In the Cartesian-Kantian-Husserlian kind of critique, knowledge itself is not problematised, what is problematised is the ways and means of knowledge. In other words, the 'how' of knowledge is problematised, but the 'what' of knowledge is left out. As a contrast, Heidegger not only problematises the relationship between consciousness and knowledge by way of setting it in the context of being, but sets being as the ground of knowledge, which makes both the ground of knowledge and knowledge aporetic and impossible in character. This ontological move dissolves both the metaphysical problem of accommodating knowledge within consciousness and the phenomenological problem of advancing knowledge through an enveloping of the world in consciousness. But it does not dissolve the problem of knowledge altogether, rather it brings out the in-comprehension of knowledge in knowing the being.

A theory that does not problematise the concept of knowledge basically aims at extending its scope and attaining certitude by way of accommodating it within the field of consciousness. This extension of the possibility of knowledge in terms of the greater role of human consciousness develops a synthetic theory of knowledge that claims universality, infallibility and authenticity in it. A critique of knowledge that fulfils this kind of an epistemic telos is modern in character and requires full justificatory devices within its fold. The truth-claims attached to such a fulfilled state of knowledge are global, as theoretically speaking, they can fulfil the goal of knowing the world in consciousness. What marks a positive description as modern in a theory of knowledge is a theory of claiming authenticity and truth of knowledge by virtue of its objective and foundational basis. Two distinct theoretical possibilities arise here: one, its support is construed and second, its need to distinguish the claim and its support as two different realm as in mental-physical distinction. But the efficacy of the theory in crucially bridging the two realms reduces a claim, singular by nature, without allowing the human subject to dissociate herself from knowledge. Rather in relation to the immediate object of knowledge, theory stands as a mediate subject. The claim *I know 'p'* in the modern sense, therefore, represents the iron rule that knowledge can't be disjointed from the knower and further, knowledge of 'p' bears within it a self-present subject in close proximity. The knower returns to 'p' with the already acquired knowledge of 'p' in this in-dissociable self-presence. The ontological commitment of such a theory of knowledge lies in ascribing knowledge to a human subject, who knows only by access to the world. Ironically, ontological commitment of such a theory of human knowledge/subject also aims at having a 'world totally independent of our knowledge' as a condition of having 'human' as the subject of the world or the ontos.

Problematisation of knowledge can begin with its own resources by setting them in the context of the world. The way Heidegger sets knowledge in the context of the world is by asking the question about being of what is and an answer to the question cannot be exhaustive, as being of what is lies beyond thematisation within knowledge. As being of knowledge stipulated as modern cannot be determined within itself, it transgresses the limits of a theory of knowledge and creates an explanatory gap. What emerges through the gap is the knowledge that knowledge of being cannot be fully exhausted, as being of knowledge cannot thematise the being of knowledge within itself. Being of knowledge overcomes the being of knowledge and the knowledge of being as well. This unthematisable knowledge of being problematises knowledge of being and inaugurates a radical undecidability about claim of knowledge. One can say that the ontology of knowledge cannot be thematised within knowledge itself and it inaugurates a difference between ontic knowledge and ontology of knowledge. This problematisation demonstrates the ontological impossibility of knowledge, which gives rise to the very possibility of the knowledge of the ontic. Further, this problematisation of knowledge problematises the whole modern project of expanding the universe of knowledge by making it compatible with human consciousness, as it shows the radical impossibility of the knowledge of the being leading to non-comprehension of being in human knowledge.[10] Unless being is comprehended, how can the project of modern knowledge in knowing the world be completed? One can term this mode of problematisation of the limits of human knowledge as postmodern as it inaugurates possibilities of being as the other of knowledge that *escapes* knowledge.

One cue for problematisation of knowledge, therefore, is asking the question about ontological commitment of a theory of knowledge. For example, the ontological commitment of the Cartesian and Kantian theory of knowledge tries to attain self-evident knowledge of the world, while the ontological commitment of a Heideggerian critique of knowledge lies in recovering the being from knowledge-as-such. Deciphering the ontological commitment of theories of knowledge helps one to understand the limits of critique involved in such theories and whether the critique problematises knowledge or not. Ontological commitment of a theory of knowledge by referring to concepts and objects can be known by the subject of its critique and how it relates that subject in its description of knowledge. Such description of knowledge gives rise to specific language in which the theory of knowledge is inscribed and a critique of knowledge can reveal its ontological commitment by making the language used in the theory as its subject of critique.

With the rise of linguistic philosophy, the critique of language, that is the concepts used in a theory of knowledge, is made the subject of critique through which the ontological commitment of the theory can be registered. Critique of concepts used in language involves the semantic presentation of these concepts and what they refer to. Semantic presentation of these concepts makes propositions about the world that need to be interpreted. Interpretation of propositions in a theory of knowledge by understanding what they refer to provides an understanding of the ontology that is in view in such theories. A critique of knowledge that accepts the semantic meaning as it is and identifies the reason behind framing certain propositions ends up by merely analysing the structure of the theory of knowledge. Such an analysis confined within the semantics of theory does not displace the theory, but brings out its ontological commitment in semantic terms. This kind of a critique could be termed as a critique within the 'given' theory of knowledge and hence it reproduces the theory in its own terms.[11] The ontology of the theory is merely interpreted in such critiques and this is what would be termed as modern as it runs contemporary with the theory itself.

Another kind of critique that interrogates the semantic structure of theory of knowledge by way of relating the references of such a theory to the context crosses the already determined descriptive context laid out in the theory. This kind of critique brings out the reason for using concepts within the theory and interprets it as a construction of theory. The critique figures out how the theory presents itself and interrrogates in theory. Such a positioning of critique in what the theory excludes, even though such an excluded domain constitutes the possibility of the theory that it critiques, overcomes the limits of the theory that it critiques. Such overcoming opens up the possibility of new interpretation and reformulation of the ontology or argues a new ontology altogether. This is what in its style presents the postmodern critique of knowledge.[12] Such a critique thwarts the modern character of the theory by enacting a problematique within the theory that displaces it; the modern characteristic would have been to retain the framework of the theory even in the case of rejecting a particular theory.

Styles of Problematisation in Richard Rorty, Jacques Derrida and Jurgen Habermas

The radical debunking of the human subject and the consequent re-interpretation of knowledge contributes to the focal tension in Rorty, Derrida and Habermas' critique of knowledge. While Rorty and Derrida formulate an impossibility of knowledge in its authentic and truthful form, Habermas rediscovers knowledge in universal 'forms of life'.[13] For Rorty and Derrida, the meaning of human action and human life cannot be known as a 'whole', but can only be known by setting it in contexts and changing these contexts. For Rorty and Derrida, the life-contexts merely demonstrate that one's concept of knowledge can neither be fixed and determined nor claim the authority to know these concepts. For Habermas, still, life and the world can be approached from a vantage point that consists of knowing life and the world and it is in this process of acquiring valid knowledge about something that an already ordained theory of knowledge can come into play.

1. Rorty takes a position upon the traditional view of knowledge. First, grounding a knower on the basis of a capacity to know, reflect or view is a metaphysical construction giving rise to two different realms, 'subjective' and 'objective', between which a relation of mutual dependence, one standing upon the other, is conceived. This mode of construction of knowing a subject in the Cartesian-Kantian phenomenological schools of thought, for Rorty, made philosophy a systematic discipline that appropriates physical reality within the mental realm and constructs a mental realm that produces a mirror of the world. This critique of a human subject and its image of an Archimedean point of view upon the world removes the 'foundational' concept of knowledge and instead relocates knowledge in the language through which human practices find an expression. Language also is removed

from its Cartesian innateness to a field of open-ended and live social interaction that creates the world for the human being and opens the world for the human being who stands upon the 'mental' and 'detached' edifice of linguistic foundations to see the world from the outside.[14]

2. As far as Derrida is concerned,[15] continuing the human subject as 'knower' produces a 'closure' in knowledge, which means holding back the never-ending play between the world and the human being by positing a finality and by returning to an origin, ground, truth or logos. Derrida calls this an ethico-theoretical decision to bring the play of oppositions to an end in order to produce a singular meaning effect by deferring the opposition that constituted the decision. The human subject as 'knower' assumes that kind of a power to make itself the subject of such an ethico-theoretical decision that goes along with the centrality of the human subject and opens up both knowledge and the human subject to an open-ended play of knowledge and the world represented in a medium of knowledge.

Exploring both these styles, one can see that there is a common ground between Rorty and Derrida in the matter of dislodging the human subject by making a critique of its Archimedean point of view (in Rorty) and by making a critique of the ethico-theoretical decision to project such a view (in Derrida). His abandoning of the human subject as a knower with an autonomous self-endowed warrant to reflect and to take a decision leads to a greater emphasis on language as a medium that acts as constitutive of and constituted by human practices in such a manner that there is an ongoing and live interplay between language and human practice. For Rorty, such interplay both limits and opens up the meanings attributed to the human practice and life so that it is neither universal nor final at a point. For Derrida, language is a possibility and he transposes this possibility of infinite structural play within knowledge itself. Again, for both Rorty and Derrida, the metaphysical and phenomenological descriptions of human knowledge is a damp squib as it essentialises, determines and fixes knowledge. Rorty abandons the human subject as a knower altogether and redescribes it in terms of possibilities within languages, while Derrida analyses the Heideggerian move to ontologise the human subject in being and finds a closure that comes through its manifestations and determinations that makes being 'a denial of its own possibilities' and a fulfilment in an absolute abundance. For Derrida, both these extreme possibilities of ontology represent a metaphysical calling of the other side and hence produce a closure. So, Derrida denies ontology by way of exploring its possibilities and exploring such possibilities in an ontology constitutes a crucial step in Derridean restriction of the play of being.

3. For Habermas, 'the paradigm of the philosophy of consciousness'[16] represents a metaphysics of essential ground/nature of experience and an omniscient subjectivity, which needs to be forsaken in order to attain knowledge. The paradigm of philosophy of consciousness puts an idealistic demand on the knower to self-referentially incorporate the conditions of knowing in theory that justifies all its formulations about the world. Abandoning such theoretical moves within philosophy makes Habermas start from the 'life world' of societies, which ironically leads him to theorise on the universal structures of the life-world in normative terms to indicate the possibility of universal and uninterrupted communicative action. The premises of such communicative action are derived in a neo-Kantian a priori form of cognition that explains what there is in the world and society.

The Controversy

At a general level, the critique of knowledge in Richard Rorty, Jacques Derrida and Jurgen Habermas is aimed at abandonment of the human subject as a knower. Rorty and Derrida problematise the concept of knowledge even after abandonment of the human subject. Both of them develop an alternative concept of knowledge, which is closer to a concept of play than to truth, finality and determinacy. Rorty advocates a concept of language that is culturally bound and which does not lay any claim to knowledge in the traditional sense, but articulates the needs of 'self' and 'community'. Contrarily, Derrida's concept of language is an interpretative move that overcomes the limits set by our knowledge of the world. He problematises knowledge and, by locating how language interlopes into the construction of human knowledge, extends it beyond the professed closure. Both Rorty and Derrida prioritise the role of language in making the 'self', 'community' and 'world', which involves for Rorty a matrix of social relationships, and for Derrida, an interminable interplay between concepts within language that give rise to a new meaning, interpretation and description of the world. Therefore, critique of knowledge in Rorty and Derrida is a problematisation of the relationship of the human subject with its knowledge claims in terms of language that acts as a medium for representation. We have characterised such a problematisation of knowledge by problematising its ontological commitment and characterised the problematisation as postmodern; since Rorty and Derrida's problematisation bears this problematisation of ontological commitment of knowledge, it is postmodern.

Contrarily, even though Habermas accepts this radical capability of language, he favours neither a culturally bound concept of language nor an infinite possibility of meanings within language. He begins from the mode of usage of ordinary language, in which speech-acts presuppose certain universally shared presuppositions of meaning and communication.

Habermas reconstructs these presuppositions. Therefore, critique of philosophy of consciousness is directed by him towards rediscovering the pragmatic presupposition in ordinary speech-acts. Knowledge is constituted by the possibility of uninterrupted communication provided by pragmatic presuppositions of speech acts. Habermas links up these pragmatic presuppositions of communication with the tripartite structural division of modern society in spheres of cognition, morality and aesthetics giving rise to three kinds of validity claims in knowledge upon language that mediates between knowledge as communicative action and spheres of modern society. He establishes a horizontal relationship between communication, language, knowledge and society in an integrated theory of modernity in which any one of the elements wholly bear the structure of the other.

For the purpose of comparing these three distinct critiques of knowledge, one can compare postmodern and modern positions with reference to knowledge as available in the texts of these three philosophers and as discussed above. The comparison will take each philosopher at a time and identify these strands within each one's writing separately.

1. As a specific problem, Rorty's abandonment of philosophy in conversation and poetry creates a critical tension within philosophy. On the one hand, Rorty suggests creation of culturally specific criterion of knowledge and interprets language with such a criterion, and on the other, he suggests an exploration into genres of literature for overcoming the bind of 'final vocabulary' in a 'poetics of self making'. Such a dichotomy in Rorty ultimately keeps 'public' and 'private' spheres strictly separate and by implication, separates 'philosophy' from 'literature'. One can advance the thesis that a search for 'common human nature' will allow us to continue with this apparent dichotomy.
2. In the case of Derrida, deconstruction as a means to overcome presence as logos and opening up a play of

'presence' and 'absence' produces a central tension in his project. On the one hand, deconstruction opens up new possibilities of meaning, and on the other, it operates within the metaphysics of presence. Therefore, the thesis raises the question, does deconstruction as critique confine itself within the circularity of presence? If it does, does deconstruction turn against itself? This thesis shall explore this problematique.

3. In Habermas, structuring of communicative action in terms of pragmatic presuppositions of speech-acts and its later interpretation in construing a 'discourse ethics' provides a holistic explanation of the relationship between human subject and communication. The central tension in Habermas' constructivism is his derivation of a normative foundation of communicative action from the life-world context, which is gradually integrated into the spheres of modernity. Thereby, the transformation of the life-world into the public sphere is increasingly developing its own transformed norms. In such a situation, does Habermas' theory of communicative action and discourse ethics explain this transformation or impoverish its theoretical tools?

Such specific problems further open up two distinct levels of comparisons. At one level, specific problems accruing from each individual philosopher's explication could be brought in parallel. At another level, the critique and debate between these three philosophers provide an exhilarating fulcrum to the problem of critique of knowledge.

1. Rorty's advocacy of a culturally rooted knowledge system closely interlinked with the use of language inaugurates a liberal community. Derrida's 'community of interpreters' shares protocols of reading and Habermas's communicatively structured community shares a common ground, but don't their ways of explanation mutually problematise each other? Rorty's grounding of a liberal community is opposed to Derrida's deconstructive practices of ongoing

radicalisation of language and knowledge situated in a community and vice versa. Habermas' normative structuring of communicative action presents the picture of a society that subdues differences into a consensus and hence reproduces the structures of status quo. The comparison will explore the incommensurability of epistemic explanation between them.

2. At another level, mutual debates between Rorty, Derrida and Habermas bring out the irresolvable problems between these perspectives. In particular, Habermas' philosophical allegation about Derrida's retrogression of enlightenment into the mysticism of monotheistic being and Rorty's critique of systematicity in Habermas' notion of consensus and Habermas' response to it by terming Rorty as 'conservative' provide cues to each philosophy for the other point of view. The latter chapters of this book will demarcate the area of convergence and difference between them.

The comparison on the above stated aspects should bring about another question: What happens to knowledge and critique of knowledge in postmodernity (as in Rorty and Derrida) and in modernity (as in Habermas)? An overview could be presented after arriving at a comparison and an open-ended answer provided to the question.[17]

Notes

1. Martin Heidegger, *The Principle of Reason*, trans. Reginald Lilly, Indian University Press, Bloomington and Indianapolis, 1996, pp. 69-74.
2. Hubert Schwyzer, "Subjectivity in Descartes and Kant", *The Philosophical Quarterly*, Vol. 47, No. 188, pp. 342-357. See p. 357.
3. David Hume, *An Enquiry Concerning Human Understanding*, 2nd ed. E. Steinberg, Hackett Publishing, Indianapolis, 1993, pp. 49-51.
4. Barry Stroud, "Kantian Argument, Conceptual Capacities and Invulnerability" in Paolo Parrini (ed.), *Kant and Contemporary Epistemology*, Kluwer, Dordrecht, 1994, pp. 231-51. See pp. 233, 234, 235.

5. One can read here the beginning of a critical disfiguring of Kant. A philosophical-hermeneutic account could be read in de Man, "Phenomenality and Materiality in Kant" in Gary Shapiro and Alan Sica (eds.), *Hermeneutics: Questions and Prospects,* University of Massachusetts Press, Amherst, 1984, pp. 121-44.
6. Edmund Husserl, *Ideas*, Vol. I, trans. W.R. Boyce Gibson, Collier Books, New York, 1962, Sec. 33, 75, 59. etc.
7. Martin Heidegger, *The End of Philosophy*, Harper and Row, New York, 1973.
8. Onora O'Neil, *Construction of Reason: Explorations of Kant's Practical Philosophy*, Cambridge University Press, Cambridge, 1989, p. 167.
9. Jacques Derrida, *Writing and Difference,* trans. Alan Bass, University of Chicago, 1976.
10. This echoes David Chalmers' Hard Problem of Consciousness in the explanatory gap between 'phenomenal states' and physical states/cognitive states as explicated in his text. See David Chalmers' *The Conscious Mind: In Search of a Fundamental Principle*, Oxford University Press, New York, 1996.
11. This is what Louise Antony calls the 'dragnet' theory of Knowledge in her essay entitled, "Quine as Feminist: The Radical Import of Naturalized Epistemology" in Louise Antony and Charlotte Witt, *A Mind of One's Own: Feminist Essays on Reason and Objectivity,* Westview, Boulder, Lolo, 1993, p. 206.
12. One good example of this style could be Donald Davidson's "A Nice Derangement of Epitaphs" in Ernest Lepore (ed.) *Truth and Interpretation*, Basil Blackwell, Oxford, 1986, pp. 433-46.
13. For ready references, one can read through Richard Rorty, *Essays on Heidegger and Others*, Cambridge University Press, Cambridge, p. 74; Jacques Derrida, *Writing and Difference*, trans. Alan Bass, University of Chicago Press, Chicago, p. 260 and Jurgen Habermas' *Postmetaphysical Thinking*, trans. W.M. Hohengarten, Polity Press, Cambridge, 1995, pp. 135-36
14. Richard Rorty, *Philosophy and the Mirror of Nature*, Basil Blackwell, 1980, pp. 357-94.
15. Jacques Derrida, *Raising the Tone of Philosophy: Late Essays by Immanuel Kant, Transformative Critique by Jacques Derrida*, ed. Peter Fenves, John Hopkins University Press, Baltimore, 1993, pp. 166-67.
16. Jurgen Habermas, *Autonomy and Solidarity: Interviews*, trans Peter Dews, Verso London, 1995, pp. 149-89.
17. The book leaves the problems in a loose and disentangled relationship without a final conclusion and only attempts at culling some tentative conclusions that are revisionary in nature.

II

Richard Rorty's Poetics of Knowledge

A Critical Revision

A Problematique of Interpretation

Richard Rorty is read as a 'non-metaphysical nominalist'[1] who uses metaphysics for validating the practice that it makes feasible.[2] This reading of Rorty gets further enunciated in labelling him as a Kantian who maintains a strict separation between noumena and phenomena in his interpretation of the world as ineffable and vacuous. This mode of Kantian bracketing of Rorty generates an explanation of sorts:

> It may be suggested here that we should read Rorty as ending up with something of a Kantian position. There is an internal pragmatic stance from which we happily use and accept realist sounding sentences, with their commitment to objectivity and world guidance and language transcendence. But then there is an external stance from which we recognise the 'merely' pragmatic function of all such sentences as we use them. Through understanding that function, we recognise that objectivity cannot be understood in the realist way, but that it is a projection of our practices. So we become internal, pragmatic, realistic and 'transcendental' linguist idealists.[3]

The tenor of such an explanation is further carried forward in affirming that Rorty's anti-epistemological and antimetaphysical stance merely espouses a non-committal liberal pragmatism. It is liberal to the extent that it endorses the 'hopes' of individuals and pragmatist to the extent that it looks for 'useful' appropriation of such hopes and despairs. Such a fixing of Rorty bears significant counter-Rortyean epistemological and metaphysical claims identified and derived from within Rortyean narrative. One such claim is that Rorty's debunking of any knowledge and truth is an aestheticised version of reality, put in anti-Rortyean terms, is merely a subscription to metaphilosophical reason, which is constituted not by its content, but by a depth-metaphysical structure. Invention of such latent, unspelt-out structures in Rorty's thought has been a mark of philosophical prudence by which Rorty's thoughts are taken to be an autonomous subjectivity, typical of assuming an Archimedean point of view of a philosopher. Much philosophical prudence goes into reading Rorty as this or that, such as two Rortys, one inferential and the other imaginative; or a Rorty who develops the notion of a subjectivity causally related to the world through its own content[4]; or a Rorty who cannot defend his liberalism because of its non-grounding in a 'community'.[5] All such readings of Rorty stem out of a basic epistemic perplexity: How can Rorty think of an 'anything goes' kind of situation by 'what is good in the way of belief' without supplying a criterion for evaluation and judgement! In other words, how can Rorty advance, reassemble, successful and useful belief/knowledge claims by undermining the basis of such claims and how can he consider them useful when these are so radically different from the intention/purpose spelt out in them? An example of this perplexity shall make the scene clearer. Rorty ordains the replacement of questions of validity and the truth of an assertion by questions about limits of community, character of encounter between human beings in our society, etc. Critics of Rorty disapprove of such a replacement on the ground that if the question of epistemic validity is replaced, how can one decide about matters of collective and community interests. But

Rorty's attempts are at relinquishment of the controversial activity of climbing out of our minds for finding 'mind-independent and language independent' reality to create an alternative field of inquiry in which one can have alternative descriptions of reality made possible through shared beliefs and practices within cultural finitude. This leap of Rorty in measuring the social relevance of epistemological questions gives primacy to a holistic and socially determined field of belief and practice, which fixes and determines the conception of reality as proposed by some scientific methods as well. A claim like 'we must, in practice, privilege our own group, even though there can be no non-circular justification for doing so' problematises what such a claim does, quite similar to that when Rorty denies the existence of determinate mind-independent reality. Such problematisation of the 'condition' on which a claim bases itself leaves open the question of criterion of truth and knowledge, even though the act of problematisation includes a conception of 'reality'.

Rorty's Interpretive Positions in Philosophy

Rorty's undermining of the basis of knowledge claim, be it cognitive, moral, scientific or evidential, is a position of openness, a position that can be construed and rejected without any authentic and/or authoritative gaze. The abandoning of the criterion of authenticity and authority makes it possible to see what sorts of belief are held in a human community without differentiating it in specialised disciplines, institutions and practices. That is how Rorty can take a Jamesian position of 'the will to believe'[6], which rejects 'evidence' as something useful to understand the world, and prescribes truth to be what is good for us to believe. Here belief acts as the fuzzy marker of the already existing relationship between the contents of belief, facts and ideas. Belief acts as a fuzzy marker because 'what is good for us to believe' is contingent and contextual, but non-derivable from any given situation, it is rather a matter of sharing the views, opinions and perspectives of others. It makes it possible to remain responsible to 'us', instead of corresponding to something lying 'out there'. The habit of thinking through certain determined references to the world outside splits and empties out both the thought and the world and also someone out of her situated place. Rorty's precise interpretive position is that what constitutes belief cannot be isolated and differentiated as a tertia from belief. But the question is does that mean a kind of subjective and autotelic closure? Rorty does not close beliefs to such a closure, but includes in it most things in space and time which are effects of causes other than human mental states. Similarly, he contends that the belief states are not the effects of something material, lest they are again supposed as two different domains, because belief about such different domains bridge them up without being caused by any of them. Again beliefs are not uncaused, even though these are not caused by the causal link between belief and world. So, what causes beliefs to be what they are? Rorty's Deweyean answer to this question is remarkable:

> As soon as we start thinking of 'the world' as atoms and the void, or sense data and awareness of the (...) We are (...) well within some particular theory about how the world is (....).?[7]

In other words, cause of belief could only be known through 'theories' about them. But Rorty's well-known position that 'theory' is a metaphor for description gives rise to a further question about cause, which is never precisely identifiable outside belief or discourse. 'Causality' here stands as a notion best described by Rorty against Dennett's programmatic use of computer software, when he talked about a blissful ignorance in picking up a programme without knowing how a computer embodies and executes the programme.[8] Rorty's fuzzy notion of causality demurs a definite one to one relational linkage to leave it open to interpretive linkages that could be drawn from possible sequences of events. Minimally, causality presupposes an interconnection without a definite categorical description that is explicitly stated in the belief that states the 'causes' as well. In other words, causes for belief and the belief itself cannot be separated as they give content to an integral description. Rorty merely hints at the possibility of a commensuration between belief and its causes within belief and its description. What Rorty arrives at is a generalised notion of belief in synonymity with 'the way things are' or with 'the way we know things', which brings forth the possibility that there could be either commensurable status of belief about things in the world or the world in general. But it is never that belief is a categorical description or a synthetic judgement about something, it is simply without these makers of certainty. It is a 'generated' notion that describes our particulars, senses, feelings, sentences, attitudes, etc. Belief is everything but a candidate for validity. This means a charitable notion of belief in which belief of one kind or one person is perfectly justified as the belief of another kind or another person.

This opening of belief provides Rorty the much needed fulcrum to move beyond the closed rationality of determination of true/false, right/wrong, good/bad by appealing to some universal criterion and enables him to look into the wider possibilities of meaningful beliefs beyond one's own epistemically verified true beliefs. How such an opening became useful can be illustrated with examples of Rorty's interpretive stances. That truth does not lie out there in some fixed objective reality, but is created through participation and communication between the subject and the object and what is held to be true in a statement is a product of such live processes is an important interpretive position drawn by Roty from Dewey's naturalism. Dewey's naturalism was transformed into an idea of such living communication by Rorty that it acquires linguistic representation to present the way a society or a community speaks of such interaction. That truth, further, does not lie in one yardstick of reality in human feelings is another mode of recasting William James in terms of the language of the human subject who takes a 'perspective' on it. This is a point of hermeneutic convergence between William

James and Dewey at which the freely construed linguistic expression emanating from the human participants are celebrated. Rorty commends such a convergence by asserting that language is a more suitable notion than experience for expressing the holistic and anti-foundationalist things James and Dewey wanted to say.

Critique of the Human Subject

Rorty develops a critique of the human subject by criticising the philosophical tradition that subjects it within theoretical frameworks. By drawing a contrast between transcendental idealist and pragmatist relativist ideas of knowledge, Rorty distinguishes the human subject from the way in which it is philosophically appropriated. The basic question of his critique can be formulated as: How do we recover the human subject from its prevalent representation within philosophical tradition? Rorty does it in three ways: (1) by a critique of the 'mind' as an essentialised feature of the human being, (2) a critique of universal human nature, and (3) a critique of confrontation. All these ways are interrelated, still one can distinguish between these three different critiques of human knowledge.

Rorty further distinguishes two forms of philosophy: First, a transcendental idealist position like the Kantian one that maps the world in the subject, and the other being the ordinary pragmatic way of relating and comparing texts with texts in order to have a useful grasp over what it says. In the first mode, Rorty identifies description of processes that generate truth and the activity of human mind to know such processes. The mind is conceived as a mirror of nature that images the reality and language must hook up that image in expressive forms. The inherent dependency relationship between the world and the mind in such a description makes pragmatists suspicious of success of such a description in the context of life.

(1) *Critique of the Human Mind:*[9] The notion of mind as an irreducible organ of human consciousness with a capacity

to know the world through mental states is critiqued by Rorty. Rorty strikes at an obnoxious distinction that states that consciousness can exist independent of bodily sensations. This gives a picture of the human being as having both an 'inside' and an 'outside'. Rorty claims that such a 'bifurcation' is essentially a creation of the 'philosophy of mind' or it is a derivative of the metaphysical property of consciousness, following Quine, who showed how what we mean by 'mental' may turn out to be a statement about a physical event or state and vice versa. This particular possibility of overlap between 'mental' and 'physical', for Rorty, could be described without a casual relationship, as required in theories of knowledge. This could be done simply by terming it as an ability to describe a mental or physical/mental state and such association of representations is a way of making a causal reference by assuming an identity/ownership over such representations. Therefore, our knowledge of the mind does not presuppose an inherently mental/physical distinction, but mixes it up with one another by way of making statements about mental/physical states in an equivocal reference to each other, the metaphysical notion of mirroring is thereby replaced by a reference to 'irreducible' mental/physical states, which are not synthesised. Such an unsynthesisable referential description of the human being in both mental and physical terms provides an anti-naturalist conception of the human being, whose states refer to both mental and physical without a possible reduction.

(2) *Critique of Universal Human Nature*: That the human being does not have any such thing as 'human nature' or an order beyond time and change which determines the point of human existence and establishes a hierarchy of responsibilities[10] is one of the fundamental philosophical insights that Rorty derives from a vision of the human being which 'insists on socialisation and thus historical circumstances, go all the way down – that there is nothing 'beneath' socialisation or prior history which is definitory of the human.'[11] Rorty identifies two kinds of description in this whole

characterisation of human beings. 'The desire for self-creation for private autonomy' dominates in the writings of philosophers like Nietzsche, Heidegger and Foucault. These writers are interested primarily in the quest for 'private perfection' in the creation of a distinctive, autonomous life. At the same time, they express their distrust over processes of socialisation which they tend to view as 'antithetical to something deep within us',[12] which is a desire to make oneself in such a way as existing language fails to describe and they ironize the stereotypical conceptions of self and personhood.

By contrast, liberal authors like Mill, Dewey, Habermas, Rawls and Isaiah Berlin are inspired primarily by their work not as a personal quest for autonomy, but as 'a shared social effort – the effort to make our institutions and practices more just and less cruel'.[13] Indeed Rorty calls these figures 'liberal' as they think that cruelty is the worst thing that we do. Now, the question is whether this desire for private perfection and the desire for attaining social justice can be brought under a single theory that explains why human beings embody these two characteristics? Rorty's answer is that such a singular representation is possible only if a theory of human nature is constructed based upon some intrinsic values and qualities. But this kind of construction will be essentialist and foundationalist. So, Rorty concludes:

> The vocabulary of self-creation is necessarily private, unshared, unsuited to argument. The vocabulary of justice is necessarily public and shared, a medium for argumentative exchange.[14]

So, the basic points that Rorty makes in this critique are two: one, no universal human nature is possible without a foundational and essentialist ground, and two, without such foundational description, 'private' and 'public' spheres can be separated. They are linguistically 'incommensurable' and no theory should unite them in coherence.

(3) *Critique of Confrontation*: Rorty identifies certain kinds of theories as confrontationist for they instrumentalise the

human subject to go with a motive to subdue other human beings and nature. He characterises this 'confrontation' in the light of those theories. Cartesian dualism, Kantian rationalism and any other theory of human subject/knowledge that calls for justification on the basis of some evidence create a situation of confrontation in which one set of knowledge-claims upheld by one set of people stand opposed to another.[15] Rorty cites some theoretical examples of this confrontation: (1) mind-body dualism that pits the human mind as an instrument to know and reduces mind to body and vice versa by granting a privileged position to one of the sides, (2) the Husserlian apodicticity of truth by bracketing the sensible world, (3) the being of later Heidegger disclosing itself in the knowledge of technology and many other such theories that aim at giving justification to its claim by way of 'correspondence to nature of things'. An agreement based upon such a justificatory nature of theory contains within itself the ingredients of an incipient conflict between what it says and the basis construed within to justify what it says.[16] Such theories cannot simply describe without a claim of truth, without a tribunal of evidence. Confrontation occurs because such theories create some pre-existent truths and ideals that are already established and that only invite a ready agreement. Rorty includes 'scientific theories' within the ambit of such confrontation, as 'normal' sciences (in the Kuhnian sense) posit an objective world out there that can be exhaustively known independent of theories about it. Such a trans-contextual and a historical abstraction in scientific theories, according to Rorty, is the height of confrontation, as it disclaims (1) any other alternative theories, and (2) the sameness of results as the criterion of confirmation in such theories decides laws of nature in rigid and final terms. For example, the fact that water is two atoms of hydrogen and one atom of oxygen combined offer the possibility of understanding its electronic configuration in its 'substantial' liquidity. Such a force of homogeneity attained through theories bases itself upon objectively generated laws that act as its Cartesian-Kantian foundation. Rorty cautions against such a closure by saying:

> The complete set of laws which enable these predictions to be made, plus complete descriptions (in atoms-and-the-void term) of all human beings, would not get the whole 'objective truth' about human beings nor the true set of predictions about them.[17]

Rorty adduces a reason for such incompleteness, when he says:

> There would remain as many other distinct sets of such objective truths (some useful for prediction and some not) as there were incommensurable vocabularies within which normal inquiry about human beings could be conducted (e.g., all those vocabularies within which we attribute beliefs and desires, virtues and beauty).[18]

What Rorty posits here is the vocabulary within which truths about the world are understood and reasons that such vocabularies are quite different and so there should be incommensurable scientific vocabularies, too. What Rorty does here is:

(1) to prioritise the ordinary practice and criterion of success available within ordinary practices; and
(2) to adopt a similar practice of characterisation in science through vocabularies describing such practices. The case of establishing homogeneity in vocabulary in order to construe the sameness of results, in Rortyean perspective, therefore, only means a sharing of similar vocabulary in practice.

Belief as the Paradigm of Knowledge

Rorty opens up two possibilities: one, the local content of an expression (vocabulary) of belief is open to interaction with other such expressions (vocabularies), and two, the possibility of such an interaction turns the expressions in language to other such expressions and thereby resists a fixed determination of meaning. But Rorty reads beliefs in relation to assertion of the beliefs and derives the self, which is just a sort of instrument in playing off various beliefs. It is not constitutive of beliefs, rather beliefs constitute it, but it plays the role of a spatiotemporal agency in playing off a host of beliefs. The self can talk about various sorts of beliefs and through these beliefs, the self can be talked about and such is the privilege of the agency in the self, nothing more, nothing less. In other words, an agency can only be an object of inquiry in a Rortyean sense,

> For us pragmatism, (...) the object of inquiry is 'constituted' by inquiry only in the following sense: we shall answer the questions, "What are you talking about and what is it that you want to find out about?" By listing some of the more important beliefs which we hold at the current stage of inquiry and saying that we are talking about whatever these beliefs are true of.[19]

Rorty spells out the absurdity of using language by way of tying it to certain fixed senses—even beliefs do not constitute those senses. Language merely provides us the much-needed direction to make sense. So, there are no makers of sense, beliefs merely bring about the necessity to make sense. The way belief is expressed in language, sense merely brings it to light. Rorty's acceptance of the Wittgensteinian notion of the 'language game'[20] is thematised in this qualified sense of making sense of our belief and not making belief through senses. But Rorty does not accept the notion of an external context to contextualise such language games, nor does he make an internal/external dichotomy[21], but considers expression itself as sense giving or acting with sense or making sense. Rorty says:

> Think of the question, "what is that worth in real money?" a parallel to the equally naïve questions, "What sentence in the real language – the language of reason or the language of nature or the language of observation – is that behavioural disposition

> an attitude toward?" or "What price of reality – reality as it really is – is that behavioural disposition directed towards?" Or "What context does that disposition really belong in?"[22]

What Rorty points out is that any amount of linguistic description of concepts of reality and meaning cannot make any sense, yet all these expressions are 'sense giving' without being able to establish a link between sense and the disposition to capture such sense. What remains, however, are these expressions described by Rorty as marks of 'sentential attitudes'. Such sentential attitudes are 'dispositions to respond in various ways to various stimuli'.

I draw an important interpretive position of Rorty from such a description of relationship between belief and its sentential attitudes: Narratives of modern epistemology such as Descartes, Kant or Husserl have been an essentialist search for meaning that overshadow our belief about the world and such narratives were necessary for bridging the chasm between subject and object, transcendental and empirical, ideal and real. Belief and its sentential attitudes help us to get rid of such coherent, validating and centred narratives. In other words, we can do without a systematically drawn out narrative of knowledge and instead go with expressions of belief. One can read Rorty's reading of the narratives of Kant, Descartes, Husserl, etc., through Rorty's alternative narratives that uncover the beliefs of these philosophers in this domain or that, justified and validated in their ways of confirmation. An important Rortyean interpretive position could be drawn from the Rortyean displacement of knowledge by belief: beliefs and sentential attitudes turn the domain of the subjective as well as the world into the way they are expressed in sentences and they can be expressed in the most creative fashion. For the subjective, such creative expressions are propelled by the desire to escape being a copy of somebody else's expressions and thereby inaugurate a process of renewing one's own self-description in such new ways. Self-identity is marked by newness of such expressions. Further, renewing expressions of self-making means evolving ways to escape being a copy of others' beliefs as well. Therefore, it means a sentential reweaving of attitudes of beliefs. Such a reweaving re-narrativises sentences into a linked up structure, but without representing something of the world, without giving it a foundational justification. Such re-narrativisation takes a fictional or poetic mode that problematises prior form of narratives like historical characters, events, languages, etc. Reweaving of belief renarrativises such forms in a constitutive mode, in which 'self' is constituted by such narration, while narrative itself reweaves belief and its prior sentential expressions. The genre in which such reweaving could take place for Rorty is poetry and he oversees a poeticised mode of self-making by constant abandoning of the literal and celebration of the metaphorical. As for the world, the way it is expressed in sentences leads to perceiving the world as a causal fiction, as that which causes the belief and, therefore, it can appear only as part of the sentential attitude. Belief about the world expressed in sentences is simultaneously caused by the world and expressed in the way the world is, that is, through the sense of belief of the world. In other words, there is no chance of a noncircular justification of one's belief, because belief about the world can be justified only in the expression of the belief.[23] Rorty interprets the situation thus:

> (.....) the antiessentialist specialised in creating this hall of mirrors effect in getting us to stop asking which is the real thing and which is the image, and to settle for an ever-expanding choice of image (.....).[24]

He interprets belief as something that does not require an external justification, but it suffices only to ask,

> "Can you fit in the belief that the litmus paper turned red (.....) with the rest of your beliefs?[25]

In other words, instead of acquiring a fit with the world, beliefs get justified by their fit with other beliefs. Rorty radicalises a notion of self as 'beliefs and desires that it has' and such a self in fitting its beliefs with other beliefs keeps on reweaving its beliefs and itself becomes a centreless web of beliefs in which its position is the position in the web. Such a talk about position in the web of beliefs engages the self in an already constituted exchange, negotiation and dialogue with others and such an engagement, for Rorty, is crucial for situating oneself within the community, which takes precedence over the search for truth. Such a situation is not a determined one, but it is a product of sufficient negotiation within a community and this involves experimentation with a number of ideas and practices. Principles that are created through such experimentation with diverse ideas and its various expressions are reminders of the practice itself.

Therefore, Rorty's interpretive position aims at retrieving something very basic in human practices, which is belief without its realisation in epistemological form. An epistemologically justified claim, for Rorty, is an impeachment of belief and for him, belief is unimpeachable by any standard. One may misread here a Diltheyean version of *Geisteswissenchaften*, but Rorty does not see any way in which something inner could be expressed in one's belief. There is no question of falling back on such inner or other areas, but one can just be free to acquire beliefs to the extent that it is impeachable, only if it does not fit. It involves interpreting one's beliefs in relation to other beliefs as well as other's beliefs.[26] Such an interpretation, in Rorty's view:

> (....) is an exciting notion only as long as it contrasts with something harder, firmer, less controversial – something like 'explanation' or 'natural science'.[27]

Rorty suggests here a move to recontextualise the interpretations given to belief and sentential attitudes, or rather suggests recontextualisation as a practice of interpretations. But context is indeed a given or determinate one. It is the possible situation in which beliefs arise and are interpreted to meet the situation. Such situations are plural, which affects in such a way that beliefs cannot be classified under one name or one content. It will become an ever-expanding and ever-changing field of heterogeneity subverting the conventional, ways of classifying it and continually crossing the limits of these enunciations. Rorty's ineluctable dictum is:

> You do not find out anything about objects at all – you just find out about how your web of beliefs and desires can be rewoven so as to accommodate new beliefs and desires. You never get outside your own head.[28]

The impossibility of finding out objects outside the texture of sentences and the web of belief is not a negative consequence of interpretation, rather it opens up the web of beliefs to possibilities of accommodating newer beliefs. It is rather a process of entering into a new set of beliefs outside one's belief set in order to expand one's own belief set. Further, it makes one not to depend too much on the validity of one's own belief in order to make one look for what others believe and thereby not become just an insider, rather dissolve the boundary between the inside and outside of one's own belief set.

This process of creating newer beliefs opens up a process of making the self, the other and the community. What is impossible for an epistemologically centred belief becomes possible in this Rortyean freewheeling of beliefs manifested through sentential attitudes and their narrativisation without a fixed centre. This also signifies ways of moving without the community and defining the community without a necessarily inherited stable past or cultural tradition, but just anchoring it on beliefs in vogue that create its own theoretical, cultural and community centred descriptions. To sum up, the Rortyean interpretive position asserts a shift from epistemologically centred view of human beings to belief centred and free conversational communities,[29] which decide through evolving styles of conversation. Rorty sheers off the idea that one can know reality as such and there is a need for justification of human beliefs on the basis of a transcultural-transvaluational criterion of truth.

'We-Intentions' as a Criterion of Knowledge

Rorty also characterises such a turnaround for the traditional problem of truth and knowledge, a turn to the problems of solidarity and practice as coincident with the postmodern abandonment of epistemology and inauguration of self-reflexivity in interpretation and social practice. He finds such self-reflexivity in some critical ways. In his own reading, a question like "What is it for a sentence to be true?" is a question about what purpose does the sentence serve and the best answer to such a question can be provided by looking into what causes such a sentence to be expressed and how that sentence expresses a conceived relation between belief, practice and their expression. In other words, the 'assertibility condition'[30] of a true sentence stems from other conditions that crop up from a certain mode of social practice and no sentence can move beyond the realm of such a practice. Rorty invokes such a criterion because he believes that nothing else can justify a sentence except the very practice of making the sentence in a coherent relationship with all other beliefs and practices and which can defend the claim made in the sentence against all 'comers' by its practitioners.

Such a broad invocation of the criterion of social practice blocks the space for separating language and world, theory and practice. This further provides a new way to orient human reason. This is the way of being particularistic to one's belonging to a 'language community', that is to a community of users of language to share particular social practices. Such living in a particular community is built around 'our sensitivity to the particular details of the pain and humiliation of others, unfamiliar sort of people'. This in Rorty's redescription is a case of living in the 'North American community'.[31] Understanding the pain of others is a discovery of the other, which is a function of 'ethnography, the comic books, the docudrama, and especially the novel',[32] and not one of philosophy. This discovery of the other brings in an empathic identification with others in some 'we-intentions', as in the pronouncement "we all want ...", where one's membership is not indicated by 'I want ...', but by 'certain historical circumstances' whereby we are under no obligation other than 'the we-intention of the communities with which we identify'.[33] Such we-intention brings out the picture of human solidarity, rather than identification with the whole of humanity.

Through this we-intention Rorty has framed his notion of moral advance by way of the recognition of others in a community that can be theorised in three ways: first, the community gives rise to its own belief, truth, norms, etc., second, members belonging to the community adopt a culture of interdependence and third, making a community that does not require a historical certitude and evolutionary development of its 'self' for its belonging to the community.

Revisiting Epistemological Objections

Some specific objections to the Rortyean frame of critique can be cited here in order to evaluate the Rortyean critique. Davidson's objection to Rorty's misuse of his notion of causal interpretation[34] of language in terms of total loss of reference to what causes beliefs, desires and sentences is an epistemic objection to Rorty's anti-realism. Davidson raises this objection because he points out that the criterion for coherence of beliefs, etc., cannot be there within language, while Rorty's pragmatic criterion of 'good', 'use' or 'success' refers to use of language in the context of practice. Rorty retains the criterion of social practice as an 'outside' of language by agreeing with the Davidsonian idea that beliefs do no represent anything. The question is how can one speak about the usefulness of some belief without making it cohere with the relevant beliefs? In other words, how can beliefs have a local content? Even if Rorty says no non-circular justification of beliefs is possible, still do belief – content – practice make a circle without basing themselves into some practice? Again Rorty connects practice with a linguistic behaviour in relation to a situation, so how can one talk about belief without referring to some situation? This perplexity becomes clearer in two of Rorty's radical interpretations. One, when Rorty interprets Davidson's notion of metaphors in the following epistemic terms:

> For Davidson, the break between the realm of meaning and *cognitive content* (the realm in which it is useful to speak of norms and intention), and the realm of 'mere' stimuli, *is just the pragmatic and temporary break* between stimuli whose occurrence is more or less predictable (on the basis of some antecedent theory) and stimuli which are not – a break whose location changes as theory changes and as concomitantly fresh new metaphors die off into literalness.[35]

Davidson's reconciliation of the break between the 'realm of meaning' and 'cognitive content' and the realm of stimuli in terms of some explanatory theory seems to be acceptable to Rorty in realising the 'metaphoric' functioning of language, which, according to him, marks 'unpredictable shifts in causal relations to other noises'. But the point to be noted here is that the way Rorty reconciles the break between the realm of content and stimuli is based upon an antecedent theory of causes that accepts such a break as something cognisable. This dilemma of Rortyean non-descript 'breaks' becomes even more explicit in his interpretation of Dummett, the second case of perplexity, when he says:

> (...) The contrast which Dummett draws between e.g. realism about tables and anti-realism about values makes no sense for Davidson. For holists, so to speak, truth is always evidence-transcendent. But that is to say that X's understanding

> of S is never manifested in the kind of recognitional abilities which Dummett envisages.[36]

Dummett's contrast between realism and anti-realism in terms of 'matters of fact' and 'truth condition' is definitely non-holist, but it explains in particular that 'the correspondence theory expresses one important feature of the concept of truth which is not expressed by the law', 'it is true that P if and only if P' and this position of Dummett is further clarified in his thesis about the implicit knowledge of a user of language in a 'theory of meaning' by virtue of which she has the ability to employ sentences in a particular way, which further means knowing the sense in which the sentence has to be employed. Contrarily the holist's notion of use of language leaves it the way it is used by choosing a certain vocabulary; holists like Davidson and Rorty do not explain how language is used. Such an unexplained interior of the notion of 'use' makes it 'evidence-transcendent', which, in other words, does not give a reason for its use except that it is used. If Rorty's pragmatism did not require any reason for using language in a certain way, what could have been the necessity of re-description? Rorty's circular holism of locating particular uses within a coherent web of belief does not address how success comes in immediate use of language, and it does not let us know how one 'succeeds' in an audience to communicate through language.[37] Rorty also creates another circle here by including the audience within 'us', the all-embracing frame of an inter-subjective agreement. Such a circularisation precisely means that the way sentences refer to the world is already appropriated within the horizon of belief and language and once such appropriation is complete, a community appears as a field of inter-subjective agreement and such a community does not require any prior theory of using language. Rorty goes paradigmatic here and adopts a circularly integrated perspective on all possible theories with which we can employ language. But when Dummett makes it clear that 'realism consists in the belief that for any statement there must be something in virtue of which either it or its negation', Rorty is not ready to incorporate such a realistic belief within his general notion of 'use', but a generalised notion of 'belief' is made to cohere with 'use' as such. Thereby, in the garb of holism, Rorty ignores ordinary ways of using language by specific references, which for him, does not count towards making our belief about the world. Doesn't Rorty go here behind our particular ways of using language in explaining all such uses in terms of belief? This sort of a position taken by Rorty magnifies and inflates the possibility of using language in hermeneutic terms such as conversation, poetry, redescription, but presents a problem for non-linguistic abilities such as 'feeling pain'. Such non-linguistic datum of pain then would be under no description as it is not causally describable. Victims of cruelty, people who are suffering, cannot have much in the way of a language. So, Rorty's liberal poets, novelists or journalists shall have to come forward to describe the pain of victims of cruelty. But the language of suffering cannot become universal, for Rorty, it shall go into the liberal ironism of satarists, novelists, etc., who are looking for 'private perfection' in order to generate sensibility about other people's pain and humiliation. More than what is done here in linguistic terms, Rorty is trying to inspire a humanistic sentimentality to suffering, without any determined programme of action. This brings in the Rortyean idea of vagueness of notions like sympathy and love, which acquire only a metaphoric description in the language of irony and poetry. If such notions remain metaphorical, it is a strange disenchantment with the world that does not advocate any form of social action. But then the question is, What is the use of such vague notions in a liberal democracy? Or how, does non-advocacy of any form of action lead to the kind of progress that heightens one's empathy towards fellow human beings to bring in a 'politics of subjectivity', which is not rationalistic, but an instilling of one kind of subjectivity at the cost of another? Postmodern bourgeois liberalism, therefore, goes by the condition of a pluralistic autonomy that celebrates the essential diversity of human beings in terms of search for private perfection. What Rorty eliminates is the idea of progress as a product of particular conditions and he makes it relative to the prevalent beliefs of a community. Apparently here, the project of postmodern liberalism shares a commonality with a non-epistemic and non-representational mode of language, but the political project of having an open, free and liberal community does not quite jibe with the philosophical project of ethonocentrism and situated knowledge that Rorty advocates.

Rorty's Poetic Relinking of Life and Language

This question about cruelty and victimisation of others in the preceding discussion is integrally linked up by Rorty with the contingency of language, the way it is made contingent in order to accomplish new modes of self-making. Such contingency finds its best expression when things that are believed to go together are put in an obstreperous relationship. This is what is precisely done by irony as a genre of writing: It expresses what is hidden as an unnoticed aspect of something that is expressed. In other words, in linguistic use, irony expresses something radically contrary to what an expression is believed to have meant and an ironic expression becomes an obvious debunking of what is meant by the expression itself. In this way, irony cannot be considered as a simple prepositional attitude that expresses this belief or that, but it is a propositional attitude that expresses the hidden implication of our belief statements. Primarily it raises doubt about one's final vocabulary of belief. Such expression of doubt in a nominalist historicist mode takes into account the vocabulary currently in vogue.

But the purpose of a ironist is not necessarily to redescribe, while the purpose of an intellectual is necessarily to redescribe the already existing vocabulary.[38] For example, Rorty's Zealots, young Hegel, Nietzsche, early Heidegger, later Wittgenstein and Derrida are engaged in an enterprise of redescription, but not in a theory of ironism. They are redescribing the older vocabulary of the Plato-Kant canon in newer terms and not just limiting themselves to its analysis.[39] The problem they raise is described by Rorty in such terms as 'How to finitise while exhibiting a knowledge of one's own finitude (...) how to overcome authority without claiming authority.'[40]

In other words, the task of redescripting attempts to overcome the dominant claim or the central motif of the older metaphysics of epistemology such that the redescription itself does not fall back in square one once again. This task of redescription, therefore, must invent new vocabularies, which is best done through irony and the seeking of private perfection. Further, such a mode of self-creation is also meant for providing a vent to understand the suffering of others.

Rorty redescribes philosophers in close connection with novelists in such ironic mode. For example, Heidegger is read with Kundera and Dickens[41] and Derrida is read with Paul de Man in their implicit connection with the postmodern critical perspective. Similarly, Nabokov and Orwell are read by Rorty in terms of philosophical disparities. Such critical juxtaposition as well as the attempt at 'private perfection', and sensitivity to the suffering of others constitute redescriptions. In an ironic way, private perfection is attained through a passive understanding and sensitivity to the pain of others in one's very self-description and yet one cannot universalise one's own language of self-construction. The moment such a language is universalised, it makes understanding of the other impossible as it is nothing more than a stereotyping of the language of others in one's own.

This aspect of exclusivity and uniqueness of the language of self-perfecting remains ubiquitous by drawing a metaphorical assuagement from another's pain and yet such a language can only be expressed as an ironic recognition of the suffering of others within one's own articulation of private perfection. This is made evident by Rorty's unique juxtaposition of Heidegger, Dickens and Kundera as a novel experiment. For him, both Heidegger and Kundera are engaged in overcoming a common enemy, western metaphysics. While for Heidegger such overcoming consists in openness to being, for Kundera, it consists in giving every individual an equal right to have a claim over truth without anyone's truth being final. Obviously, Rorty sees greater prospect in what Kundera opens because that will go into stabilising a Dickensian crowd of eccentrics rejoicing in each other's idiosyncracies, curious for novelty rather than nostalgic for primordiality. One can read here a Rortyean redescription of both Heidegger and Kundera in Dickensian terms, an apparent meeting of two different purposes interrupting each other to produce what Rorty calls 'the democratic utopia' made synonymous with 'the novel' in Rorty's redescription. Further, Rorty ironises the Heideggerian project of the overcoming of metaphysics by putting it in mutual cross-recognition of each other's attempts at affirmation and expression of themselves. Such an actually existing mutual recognition of being in the self is an overcoming of metaphysics for Heidegger,[42] while for Kundera, it is a sequence of discoveries, and for Dickens, it is a refusal to fall under any moral typology.[43]

The irony lies herein, that which nihilates the very possibility of having a consistent self itself emerges as a possibility for making what it nihilates. This points to the existence of a thoroughly relativised and decentred notion of self, which is neither socially constructed nor a riposte of first person subjectivity.[44] Rather, self is conceived to be an entity caught within the web of communication. It emerges as and when the communication reaches a set of shared ideas about each other. Self does not acquire autonomy independent of this interpersonal and social communication, while the desire for reaching a point of uniqueness and perfection on its own stands in contradiction to the very process of its emergence. Rorty interprets this contradiction not as dialectical horns of opposition, but as two distinct modes of self-creation: one, the desire for private perfection, and the other, the ways of satisfying the needs of others. The two modes are not in conflict as private perfection and responsiveness to the other are distinct in their very affirmation.[45] Private perfectionists assume a second to none, unique image of oneself, specific to one's characteristics a capacity to harness the imagination about oneself; while responsibility towards another requires covering an area of social imperfections, the best way of representing which takes the form of an artistic creation of the social world in which one's self is not inflicted with pity for others.[46] In other words, self-creation involves not only private perfection, but also a capacity to evolve a language that captures the pain that others have. In contrast to a metaphysical notion of self in which the belief, emotion and states of being flow from some abstract standard, Rorty developed a notion of self that does not bank upon a subscription to a fixed moral or epistemological standard, but depends on the capacity to create uniqueness and responses to others. This is a minimal notion of self that is artistic:

> The tender, curious artist (....) has time for other people's fantasies, not just his own.[47]

Rorty redescribes this possibility of discovering an aesthetic out of ordinary senses in terms of freeing language from the metaphysical and moral concepts of the author such as goodness, but does not accept the prevalent notion of aesthetic as a matter of form and language, rather than 'content and life'. He redescribes aesthetic as that form of inquiry or curiosity that privileges 'content and life' over 'form and language' and such a privilege of content and life emanate in such a way that:

> we are more likely to notice the joys or the sufferings of one person if our attention is directed to it by the surprising indifference of another person.[48]

Therefore, Rorty's notion of the aesthetic hinges upon a clear sense of understanding the suffering of others and in that sense, Nabokov only partially serves Rorty's pragmatic ends as he believed that 'time and causality are hoaxes'. Similarly, Rorty's reading of Orwell and his *Nineteen Eighty Four* does not fix him as an intellectual who is 'a realist philosopher's defender of common sense against its cultured, ironist despisers',[49] but as one who sought an imagined future of human dignity, freedom and peace, and he framed a story to imagine such a future from the actual present of cruelty. Rorty celebrates such a possibility, no matter how befogged it is, but terms it as a utopia in which human solidarity is achieved 'not by inquiry but by imagination'.[50]

What Rorty drives home is the pragmatic necessity of arriving at that form of solidarity which brings together individuals within a community of sharing together, in which life shall be free from the repression of freedom. This gets a philosophical redescription in Rorty's conceptualisation of post-Nietzschean philosophy that inscribes a Deweyean strand of believing only in concrete social practices. Such a strand is revealed in Rorty's reading of Derrida in juxtaposition with Paul de Man. Derrida's deconstruction of 'presence' as interpreted by de Man as 'presence of a nothingness' gives Rorty his pragmatic take that language functions differently from the phenomenal world[51] and recognition of meaning is conceived by him as a capacity to substitute sensible signs for the latter, and so on indefinitely,[52] which links up use of language with the possibility of renewal of self and ultimately to a conceivable solidarity of all those who are engaged in the search for such a 'perfection for the self'. This again accounts for the ironic use of language in a nominalist-historicist mode of understanding the 'other' with an ingrained possibility of a renewed mode of self-creation. Such an ironic use of language creates the condition of an everlasting flux in our sensibilia in order to act as a 'basic' to understanding of the very phenomenal world itself. This is how Rorty combines the Derridean notion of deconstruction with the de Manian notion of void to emerge at the fluctuous character of language capable of redescribing the whole of human existence.[53]

'World Well Lost'

This shows that the 'world' cannot be conceived as something like a substratum because it is already intertwined in our responses and behaviour, that is the way we act. There are no residual 'posits' that accumulate through such interaction, they simply arise in our responses. We understand the world as an outcome of coherence of all such responses that produce a sense of its totality, which lies only within our conceptualisation. In other words, we look for a fit between our various impressions and beliefs without really having an already endowed potential for conceiving a fit. The fit comes through many contingencies, such as contemplation about each other's behaviour, experience of unaccountable events. In Rorty's words:

> (....) The world is either the purely vacuous notion of the ineffable cause of sense and goal of intellect, or else these planks in the boat which are at the movement not being moved out.[54]

This echoes Rorty's familiar point about causal description of the process of forming beliefs and expressing them in language and it is such a process a whole that makes something as a concept in a context. There cannot be a concept which is context independent and we cannot divide the world into those objects that are context-independent and that are context-dependent. This further shows that there cannot be any context independent object lying out there or a state of consciousness transcendent to the context by virtue of which something could be true.

The claim of necessary connection between statement of knowledge and the causal factors is an inferential relationship that cannot be established without losing the linguistic character of the statement. Rather such an inferential relation will bring back an 'inferential theory of truth' that cannot establish causes asserting something as true or holding it as true.[55] Conversely, Rorty coalesces 'truth', 'justification' and 'evidence' in the transition from the non-propositional state to the propositional state and a theory of reference/existence cannot explain this transition.[56] Therefore, Rorty contends that a theory of truth based on real reference loses its explanatory capacity precisely for the reason that what counts as evidence for a particular statement to be true cannot emerge into a general theory of correspondence or of evidence or of the whole of language. This is what Rorty calls a 'blind spot' in the scene of a relationship between language and the world and he prescribes an open-ended interpretation of the relationship:

> (......) One can epistemologise meaning by tying it to the given, or one can epistemologise truth by tying it to justification, but either tie-ups will lead either to scepticism or to extravagantly complicated, ultimately unsuccessful, efforts to evade scepticism. Either will lead us back into the maze of blind alleys which is the representationalist tradition. So the thing to do is to marry truth and meaning to nothing and nobody but each other. The resulting marriage will be so intimate a relationship that a theory of truth will be a theory of meaning, and conversely. But the theory will be of no use to a representation of what people do, rather than of a non-causal, representing relation in which they stand to non-human entities.[57]

In other words, there is no coherent way to derive 'the norms that govern our intentional attributions' and especially to derive it from some context-independent and neutral phenomenon and then turn it into a coherent theory of truth, reality and knowledge.

Notes

1. David L. Hall, *Richard Rorty: Prophet and Poet of the New Pragmatism,* SUNY, Albany, 1994.
2. Ibid.
3. Frank B. Farrell, *Subjectivity, Realism and Postmodernism: The Recovery of the World in Recent Philosophy*, Cambridge University Press, Cambridge, 1994, p. 124.
4. David L. Hall, Ibid.
5. Communitarian critics of Rorty point out his notion of an open-ended and ungrounded 'community', which cannot ground any normative discourse like liberalism. This kind of critique is available in Norman Geras, *Solidarity in the Conversation of Humankind: The Ungroundable Liberalism of Richard Rorty*, Verso, London, 1995.
6. Richard Rorty, *Objectivity, Relativism and Truth: Philosophy Papers,* Vol. I, Cambridge University Press, Cambridge, 1991, p. 126. Henceforth, *ORT.*
7. Richard Rorty, *Consequences of Pragmatism*, University of Minnesota Press, Minneapolis, 1982, p. 14. Henceforth, *COP.*
8. Richard Rorty, "Against Unity" in *Wilson Review*, October 1998.
9. Richard Rorty, "Persons without Minds" in *Philosophy and the Mirror of Nature*, Basil Blackwell, 1980, pp. 70-127.Henceforth, *PMN.*
10. John McCumber, "Reconnecting Rorty: The Situation of Discourse in Richard Rorty's Contingency, Irony and Solidarity", *Diacritics* 20:2-19, p. 8.
11. Richard Rorty, *Contingency, Irony and Solidarity*, Cambridge University Press, Cambridge, 1989, p. xiii., Henceforth, *CIS.*
12. Richard Rorty, *CIS*, p. xiv.
13. *CIS*, p. xiv.
14. *CIS*, p. xv.
15. Richard Rorty, "Philosophy Without Mirrors" in *PMN*, pp. 357-94.
16. *PMN*, pp. 159-60.
17. *PMN*, p. 388.
18. *PMN*, p. 388.
19. *ORT*, p. 90.
20. Richard Rorty, *Essays on Heidegger and Others*, Cambridge University Press, Cambridge, 1991, p. 23. Henceforth, *EHO.*
21. For example, Akeel Bilgrami maintains an 'internalist' and 'externalist' perspective on belief, meaning and knowledge. See Akeel Bilgrami, *Belief and Meaning*, Basil Blackwell, Oxford, 1992.
22. *ORT*, p. 98, n. 9.

23. *ORT*, p. 139, 83.
24. *ORT*, p. 100.
25. *ORT*, p. 101
26. Supra note 23 above.
27. *ORT*, p. 102.
28. *ORT*, p. 101.
29. *COP*, p. 165.
30. Rorty abolishes the distinction between assertibility conditions and truth by way of a kind of semantic holism that resists such a distinction.
31. Richard Rorty, "Postmodernist Bourgeois Liberalism" in *ORT*, pp 197-202.
32. *CIS*, p. 111.
33. *CIS*, p. 111.
34. Frank B. Farell, *Subjectivity, Realism and Postmodernism: The Recovery of the World in Recent Philosophy*, Cambridge University Press, 1994, p.19.
35. *ORT*, pp. 198-9. Underlining mine.
36. *ORT*, p. 197.
37. Uwe Staienhoff, "Truth Vs. Rorty", *The Philosophical Quarterly*, Vol. 47, No. 188, 1997, pp. 358-61.
38. *CIS*, pp. 83, 120.
39. Nominalist-historicist narration simultaneously undermines metaphysics and 'past' as history, while it upholds a redescription of culture and history in terms of current contingencies of public life. These ideas are fully explicated throughout *CIS*. Characterisation of Rorty's arguments as a nominalist historicist is enframed in David L. Hall, Supra note 1.
40. *CIS*, p. 105.
41. *EHO*, pp. 66-82.
42. *EHO*, p. 76.
43. *EHO*, p. 72.
44. *CIS*, p. 159.
45. *CIS*, pp. 155-56.
46. *CIS*, p. 158.
47. *CIS*, p. 159.
48. *CIS*, p. 165.
49. *CIS*, p. 172.
50. *CIS*, p. xvi
51. *CIS*, p.115.
52. *CIS*, p. 115.

53. *CIS*, p. 117.
54. *COP*, p. 15.
55. *ORT*, p. 148.
56. Richard Rorty, "Is Truth A Goal of Enquiry? Right Vs. Davidson", *The Philosophical Quarterly*, Vol. 45, No. 180, 1995, pp. 281-300. See pp. 285, 289, 295.
57. *ORT*, p. 154.

III

Play of Presence and Absence

Derrida's Project of Deconstruction

Knowledge as Presence

Jacques Derrida conceives of knowledge within the metaphysics of presence, which means a reduction to an essence, being or concept. Derrida locates the construction of such notions as 'essence', 'being', 'concept' and 'truth' – values assigned to them—as an affirmation of the presence of something in it which confirms the relationship between the subject and the object. Derrida further locates the specific way in which such a relationship is instituted within the discourse of philosophy. Derrida locates such an institution as an inevitable consequence of philosophy in search of the origin of a concept or an object which brings in a reference relation and a statement of fact to which the subject and the object stand in a stable relationship. A philosophical discourse construes a set of such relationships, which aims at exhausting possible modes of knowing the world and accommodates them by a thread of reason that explains the mutual relationship between the subject and the object. Derrida terms such self-explanatory reason that justifies and explains the presence of something to itself as a 'closure', which assumes a metaphysical form by establishing a regular law of relationship between the subject and the object. Derrida explains the character of closure by its character of 'invagination' of the relationship between the subject and the object within the discourse, which he further explains in terms of an auto-affection of knowledge taking place within the law of essence or truth.[1] An auto-affection is the possibility of repetition of the capacity to represent something as always present to itself, a repletion of the same from the same self-sameness, which can take place within philosophical discourse. Representation of facts through a stable relationship produces a determined space of presence bound by a flawless repetition of the same that fixes the limits of 'knowing' within the discourse. Derrida highlights this circle of auto-affection as the key to understand the metaphysical construction of reality as the repetition of the self-sameness, which is broached in phenomenology in its search for first principles and gives an ultimate foundational status to the 'being' of all forms of existence. Such a circle of auto-affection limits the possibility of knowing and only in the case of belonging to the circle are the conditions of knowing satisfied. The most suitable candidate for such a circle, for Derrida, is metaphysics, within which the founding oppositions of philosophy, the form and the world, the sensible and the intelligible are instituted.[2] Even phenomenology in its double movement of returning to the concrete and discovering the first principles of knowing the concrete, gives rise to a double metaphysics of essence and phenomenon.[3] Ontology's presupposition of being further inscribes the metaphysical necessity of the first principle within the discourse of philosophy. In recapitulating all these, Derrida captures the tendency to attain a unitary closure within metaphysics by various forms of philosophical inquiry, which inscribes and re-inscribes itself within the discourse of metaphysics. Derrida unveils two distinct historical movements in such repeated inscriptions: one, a Nietzschean moment of active forgetting of the origin, and the other, a Heideggerian nostalgia for the forgotten origin and its recalling. Further, Derrida diagnoses a constant play between these two moments in discursive metaphysics in the form of a binary mutuality. But the complementary of these two moments marks a perpetual absence, which taken singly each tries to meet, while both of them fall into an invaginated abyss of a stable origin as conceived by metaphysics. Such simultaneous belonging and non-belonging guard the non-present origin, which transcends the current determination of being and which is transgressed in the determination of the present.

These moments of forgetting and recalling of the origin give rise to a double movement of attempting a breakthrough towards what is beyond it and at the same time trying to remain within the discourse. A breakthrough is obviously an undoing of the conditions of possibility, while remaining within the discourse will mean a re-inscription of the impossibility of the conditions of possibility, that is the presence of the origin within the discourse. It would mean a displacement of the conditions of possibility into something radically different as well as an impossibility of replacement of such conditions of possibility corresponding to the double movement. Displacement of the conditions of possibility signifies an opening towards something else, while the impossibility of its replacement implies a certain closure. As far as the impossibility of replacement is concerned, Derrida conceives of it as a consequence of reduction of general context into a particular representation, metaphorically called a moment of blindness of the conditions of possibility. The metaphysical notion of 'presence', for example, gives rise to such a moment of blindness when the being of presence must be precomprehended in making itself present. So, in answering any question like "What is something X?", the being of X is precomprehended in the very question, 'What is?' This calls for a radically different character of X with which X is identical. The being of X acting as the condition of possibility for asking the question displaces the condition of possibility to something else, and at the same time irreplaceability of the being of X forbids any movement towards anything else. The double movement within the question, therefore, puts the very condition of possibility of being under question, which can in no way be answered within the possibilities of alternation and sameness. One can infer that asking such a question, 'What is?', is a suspension of being as a condition of possibility into a permanently awaited movement of its realisation that calls for its present displacement, while it is present as a fixed moment calls for asking a question about its present only, which is a suspension of the present itself. This mode of differential structuring of concepts into 'being' and its dismantling to further concepts is not given within metaphysics, even though both are grounded as origin and their relations unveiled through dismantling and construction which indicates an essential conditioning of concepts through destruction of their origin and their relationship with other concepts. But what this destruction should accomplish is a dual differential structure of 'destruction-reduction' and 'destruction-construction', the former culling together origin and concept and the latter culling together old concepts and new formations. Between these two structures, there is a moment of rupture that breaks the link between the ground and the concept by presenting a simultaneous act of grounding and un-grounding that go together, mutually interrupting and intervening. The outside of a metaphysical determination interrupts the coherence of the conceptual chain and breaks out into a vast and sweeping emergence of 'new', the wholly other. The movement of destruction-reduction, in which concepts are reduced to origin through dismantling, is an emergence of an origin ever negated in the act of destruction, which supposedly is an act to recover itself. The recovery of an origin is, therefore, a negation of it in the structure of the discourse. Between these two movements of recovery and constitution, there is a permanent breach, [4] a breach between the origin and its annulment in the chain of conceptual relationship. Derrida insists that philosophy in its relative autonomy would like to maintain a kind of balance between forces that generate these two movements. One, Derrida raises a deeper methodological question, can there be a destruction of the metaphysical discourse that suspends being into something present such that being could be recovered as an origin? Or, could there be a certain exteriority to metaphysics with respect to the presence of being, an exteriority in general in which both origin as the ground and what is grounded can be expressed?

A Discursive Characterisation of Presence

Derrida answers this question from his generalised notion of exteriority, which is not a passage from interior to exterior, it can only mean a displacement of the limit and closure of the discourse of metaphysics. What it displaces is the complicity of metaphysics in self-sufficiency of concepts and their self-relation to themselves, which produce the determination of limits of a discourse.[5] Concepts attributed with such characteristics demonstrate the grounding of concepts into themselves, which can act as the ground from which metaphysics obtains and retains its origin. In the reflexive movement of the concepts back to their ground, there is destruction of conceptual machinery while grounding different moves to break through a radically different ground. If these two movements are possible, the ground qua origin grounds concepts, while the ground qua relation ungrounds concepts into newer concepts. Derrida explains this process in terms of constituting and dislocating the concepts, both of which occur simultaneously. What Derrida points out is that the self-grounding of the concepts cannot account their ungrounding, while their ungrounding calls for a different concept altogether. What this process produces is a difference or a differential structure in which concepts designate presence. But ground as origin marks an original or fundamental presence, while ground as relation marks an infinite deferring of the presence into something other, an other that marks an absence, interrupting the other by trying to speak of contradiction without any contradiction, that is by way of a self-transposition of one movement into another, that is the move of destruction-reduction turning into its opposite of construction and then the movement of destruction-construction turning into its opposite of destruction. This is the process of reflexive determination of the negative unity of the contradiction within the realm of knowledge, as if knowledge is constituted by such a unity. Derrida characterises this unity as a metaphysical neutralisation of a contradiction through a logic of constitution, which is trapped into a kind of circle that describes 'the form of the relation between the history of metaphysics and the destruction of the history of metaphysics'.[6] Yet this circle does not signify a limit bordering a 'homogenous field', but a more twisted structure[7] that is constituted by a break between the grounds of its possibility and alienation of the ground into a discourse.

This breached structure of discourse gives rise to a notion of constitution that generates a speculation, a speculation that engenders concepts of production, synthesis, unity by a threatening gesture of incision. But this incision parts away the difference only in order to circumcise[8] them into the possibility of a self-consistent discourse, which can act as 'the self-giving evidence of the present or presence of sense to a full and primordial intuition'.[9] But the breach shows that there is an irreducible abyss or non-presence constitutive of presence kept repressed under the 'ethico-theoretical act that revives the decision that founded philosophy in its platonic form[10] and further reduced to an exterior in the form of a conceptual opposition between evidence and non-evidence.[11] This is what Derrida locates as metaphysical and as an 'obstinate desire to save presence and repetition'. But circumscribing presence within the discourse also implies a power to exclude and circumcise and a killing power. But the ethico-theoretical act of circumcision simultaneously guards itself from a metaphysical commitment to circumcise presence from its exterior, and rather circumcises this with caution:

> There must be circumcision, circumcision of the word, and it must take place once, precisely, each time one time, the one time only.[12]

Through this act of circumcision of exteriority, a total blurring between representation and reality takes place. What Derrida discloses from such an act of blurring is that the possibility of breach, acting as a primordial mark or an originary possibility of repetition[13], and the 'dissymmetric, hierarchically ordered space' of discourse, constituted by some conceptual dyads, signifies 'presence' and an exterior of 'non-presence', producing a non-homogenous oppositional space. Such a space flowing from the primordial possibility of repetition is filled with 'marks' of breach. The ethico-theoretical privileging of presence has to, therefore, figure such marks within its conceptual arrangement in such a manner that it can provide a self-sufficient explanation for the institution of presence. The figurative discourse of philosophy must, therefore, yield to provide a field for such marks to be inscribed on its body, which is an ethical must, a must that follows from its decision of not losing the presence. This primordial originary mark of breach and its circumscription into a discourse must be traversed by a number of forces that incise its internal space into a differentiated space.

Sign, Structure and Presence

The differentiated space is a space for governing the discourse within which the circumcision of the presence produces an exterior which has a structural possibility of being weaned from the concrete in general falling in the exterior. Derrida further strengthens the notion of circumcision by way of relating it to the condition of possibility of the discourse of knowledge. What such a discourse excludes is precisely, for Derrida, the condition of possibility of knowledge. Though the question about condition of possibility is a transcendental question, it interrupts the discourse by way of marks of difference invaginated within and yet generating a 'play' that can extend structurally to the infinite possibility of a polysemy. This transcendental condition of possibility produces an immanent semantic inexhaustibility that acts as a structural necessity[14] marked in the space of difference. Derrida describes such a structural necessity thus:

> In the recoiling of the blank upon blank, the blank colours itself (...) affecting itself ad infinitum – its own colourless, even more invisible, ground (...) in the act of inscribing itself on itself indefinitely, mark upon mark, it multiplies and complicates (...).[15]

Such a structurally infinite production of blanks to marks upon marks is indefinitely repeated within the other, which is a primordial structure of repetition that makes it possible for a mark to repeat infinitely. This infinite repetition takes place within the possibility of reference to other marks, which necessarily dispossesses itself away from itself, toward the other infinitely. The perpetual repetition of marks to the point of referring the other produces a structure of generalised indication, which constantly puts the minimal identity of signs into question. This putting of signs into question through constant reference to other signs itself constitutes the force of an abyssal structure. Derrida construes such an abyssal structure in terms of re-mark, a repetition of marks within difference as inscription in general, which determines positions and relations between the marks without governing the configuration within which a mark is just inscribed. In recovering the origin, reduction of the discourse leads to such inscriptions in general, which is not the annulment of the origin. The possibility of inscription in general represents an irreducible plurality in contrast to the unique origin, the origin that is simultaneously made possible and impossible within the plurality of inscriptions and, therefore, origin and its constitutive operation go through such a plurality, which only has an abyss. Derrida describes such an abyssal structure thus:

> In such a structure, which is a non-fundamental one, at once superficial and bottomless (...) it passes into the other.[16]

This passage into the other is passage into a mark, which marks the absence of itself into the presence of an other, which itself is again an absence of the other. Derrida construes this notion of 'absent-present' in a positive sense of the notion of 'sign' that represents presence in absence in its graphics. Therefore, the structure of inscription is a structure of grapheme in general. But such graphics as marks and re-marks lose their heterogeneity the moment they begin signifying, that is getting marked in in-between spaces. Because of re-marks produced as a marked mark, each mark in its reference to the other and deportation to the other must get re-marked in the fold of its disappearance or effacement. In other words, it is the effacement of marks that acts as the transcendental condition of possibility in an abyssal plurality making the mark incapable of retaining its identity, but getting folded into the re-mark, which designates it now. Derrida locates the fold or the angle of the re-mark as the undecidable play between the 're-of' the repetitions of mark and the re- of the re-marked double of the mark within which the discourse of metaphysics situates its notion of knowledge and truth. But such situation presupposes the ideal and recuperable repetition of concepts that constitute the discourse and this acts as a condition of possibility of the discourse. This condition of possibility of an ideal and recuperable repetition of concepts stands for an oppositional relationship with the primordial repetition of difference in the infinite field of inscription/graphemes in general. Rather the condition of possibility of an ideal repetition reduces the difference into sameness. The permanently repeatable meaning of signs is expressed in the elimination of difference in repetitions of the signs of the permanent meaning. The possibility of repetition simultaneously constitutes the permanence and negates the permanence into difference produced through repetition. Such permanently constituted meaning of a sign eliminates the originary structure of repetition of the sign, which is the primordial condition of possibility of permanent meaning. Derrida remarks:

> (...) There are two ways of eliminating the primordiality of the sign (...) philosophy eliminates signs by making them derivative; it annuls reproduction and representation by making signs a modification of simple presence. But because it is just such a philosophy which is, in fact, the philosophy and history of the West – which it has so constituted and established the very concept of signs, the sign is from its very origin and to the core of its sense marked by this will to derivation or effacement. Thus, to restore the original and non-derivative character of signs in opposition to classical metaphysics, is by an apparent paradox, at the same time to eliminate a concept of signs whose whole history and meaning belong to the adventure of the metaphysics of presence.[17]

The adventure of the metaphysics of presence leads to a distinction between signs that has no permanent signified and signs that permanently identify a specific signified. The signs that do not have significance are called 'merely indicative' and knowing subject experiences it as 'presence'. The signs that have fixed meaning act as the possibility of repetition. These signs are called expressive signs. It is quite paradoxical that indicative signs are repeated and it assumes the possibility of bearing certain fixed meaning just as the expressive signs do. Expressive signs are non-derivative, and they give rise to a fixed meaning that cannot retain its non-derivational character without being repeated while every repetition assumes an indicative function. Derrida further carries forwards this blurring of distinction between indication and expression in the process of repetition and points out that:

> Husserl himself gives us the means to think this against what he says(...). A sign is never an event, if by an event we mean an irreplacable and irreversible empirical particular (...). This

> identity is necessarily ideal. If this necessarily implies a representation: as Vorstellung, the locus of ideality in general, as Vergegenwartigung, the possibility of reproduction in general, and as representation, in so far as each signifying event is a substitute (...). Since this representative structure is signification itself, I cannot enter into an effective discourse without being from the start involved in unlimited representation.[18]

Therefore, elimination of the concept of indicative signs as presence into expression and the concept of expressive signs into representation leads us to the position that expression as signification embeds representations and this leads to the elimination of the distinction between 'representation' and 'reality'. Derrida takes the process of elimination of primordiality of signs to a logical end in order to show that founding conceptual oppositions between real and representation, effective and fictitious, do not stand in the case of signs bearing the function of representation. This further incorporates representation as a function of a primordial structure of repetition available in the discursive space constituted by perpetual re-marking of the graphics. This incorporation of representation into the structure of repetition marks it as a structure of signs, marked by difference between them. This structure of signs, henceforth, would always displace presence into representation, which is further displaced into the difference present in between signs, themselves markers of absence of something present within such structure of signs. Whether signs would function to present objects or they would represent them is undecidable and this undecidability would destabilise signs from bearing a fixed meaning relationship between them.

Presence, Representation and Difference

Once again, starting from the project of elimination of difference between presence and representation, origin and structure marks, one can go into the science of linguistics and semiology, none of which adduced a secondary and derivative status to signs. In Saussurean linguistics, sign is given its position within a chain of signifiers, which in totality determines its meaning and position. Both the meaning and position are fixed by the totality of signification and by the exchange and combination between them. But such exchange and combination are treated as two sides of 'one and the same production'. This notion of unity produced through a chain of signifiers is the crux of Saussurean linguistics, in which a signifier acquires a fixed Significance through its presence in the totality. Derrida shows that the totality of signification is constituted by the difference between arbitrary signs, which affect the totality, and totality in itself is never present in and of itself without this difference. Derrida gives a special reference to this effect of difference, which further produces a representation without any pre-given relationship of knowledge. This representation further affects a causality. All these series of effects are differential in character in such a manner that retracting its precedent cause only produces a difference between the representation and what is represented, which are hierarchically arranged in the functioning of ordinary language.

This shows the idealising role of signs and its relevant negativity, both of which work within the sign to unsettle the sensory receptions. An idealisation that follows is the concept of a physical ideality, which is displacement of reality or spatial criterion into some hierarchies. This movement of idealisation summarises the entire metaphysics of presence, a certain organisation of functions that philosophy has called 'meaning'. Further, this idealising move prescribes a metaphysical way of thinking of the being. One example of this is humanism, which re-appropriates being 'in the thinking of the truth of man' to ensure a transition between metaphysics and humanism via a universal following of various moves of idealisations. In Derrida's words:

> 'Being' and language – the group of language – that the we governs or opens: such is the name of that which assures the transition between metaphysics and humanism via the we.[19]

The question that should be asked at this point is, How could the construction of a metadiscourse of humanism and metaphysics undermine the primordial structure of repetition of marks that signify nothing? One obvious Derridean answer is, by privileging concepts, the negative image of a differentiated space of mark is inscribed in the concept itself, as concepts are conditioned upon such a field of heterogeneous marks. So, the concepts that represent a unified presence to itself are interrupted by the non-presence produced by those marks. This interruption constitutes the present and 'divide the present in and of itself'[20] and thereby divide the concepts into presentation to itself and presentation to the other. Such a division extracts a reduced predicative trait held in reserve by the concept in presenting its content to itself. This regulated extraction of the predicate enables the concept to represent and this is a sort of displacement of the limits and closure of the concept within the discourse that gives rise to it. This acts as a lever of intervention[21] such that interventions produce another structure of a derivative discourse that borrows its artifacts from the previous one and yet makes a difference.

This marking of a difference will always bear the trace of the previous predicates, which are newly predicated in the discourse derived from any pre-given conceptual structure. The two discourses grow in an interlaced manner such that neither of them neutralises the force of the concepts contained in them, but chooses to interlace the usable parts of the concepts. By doing so, the two discourses thwart the illusionary possibility of moving out of their field of concepts; rather they engrave concepts in a newer mix. Structuring two fields of discourse in such a manner that one always bears the trace of the other in a constitutive sense mark a rupture in the conceptual interior of discourse. Such a rupture lays open the closure of discourse into a structure of differences.

This structure of difference displays two characteristics: one, regulation of conceptual predicates refers back to the a priori difference that marks a space of inscription. Such a space of inscription further exhibits a double movement: a movement of designation or position by which the field of their production gets blended with the space unfolding between marks of the series; and a movement of re-mark that marks the space between repeated marks and marks that are already there. Such a movement represents marks in a series and marking of the space between marks in that series is coloured by the recoiling of the mark on itself and onto some other marks. Such a re-marking of the space in-between in the act of recoiling and passing on to other marks makes the space of inscription inexorable. What one has to understand is that a re-mark is not simply a recoiling repetition, but a structure of self-reference as well as reference to the other. Therefore, in the process of re-marking, the marks represent themselves and this representation withdraws them towards other unmarked marks to make them represent, which further marks them withdraw ceaselessly.

Such a structure of representation functions as a structure of signs that functions like linguistic signs, though it is more primordial than the linguistic signs. This primordiality makes possible representation, which merely strives for an identity of signs, which is derived from this basic structure of difference. But the primordial structure of signs derives ideality from repetition and so there is a priori effacement of the sign in order to emerge into re-mark, a doubling of the mark that supplements the already effaced mark. The effacement makes possible the supplementing function of a re-mark. This is like a structure that marks presence between possible and impossible, a structure that is without a non-self-identity, in which identity is always affected onto its re-marking. The supplementary addition of the mark to its other un-marked correlates is a simultaneous production of 'blank', an effacement and a delayed restitution of one effaced sign on another, to be effaced to a different one. This structure of supplement is a structure of reappropriation of the withdrawn signs in an outside of re-mark that points to an infinite substitution, 'in-the-place of-itself', an auto-affection that is delayed infinitely. The presence achieved through such supplements is an auto-affection that structurally haunts the absence of a stable presence, the mode in which the self affects itself. Such an auto-affection is unmediated except by its own act of designation that endlessly subverts recoiling into one's own self by an openness towards an unmarked exteriority in general. Derrida considers this primordial structure of repetition a fecund source of episteme, the source of non-identity, the trace of erasure of the identity which takes place in the form of 'protowriting (...) at the origin of sense'.[22] This protowriting takes place in the traces of erasure of signs into an ideality producing re-mark, a non-sense, an impossibility to coincide with itself. This draws a reference to Derrida's famous allusion to Freud's idea of deferment of pleasure in which pleasure is delayed by postponement of satisfaction manifested in traces that are neither pleasure nor displeasure, but just unconscious traces on the psyche that cannot be named within presence or absence.[23] Such a process of perpetual deferment of the final satisfaction or acquiring of the signified brings in a structure of folds. Derrida asks this question, What is the effect of such a structure on subjectivity or rather the effect of subjectivity as it is produced in the structure?

Derrida answers the question in two ways: one, the idea of supplementing, that is adding and substituting, that goes on at the protowriting follows a mode of marking every position, and two, such marks play the role of re-inscribing any discourse/signification into a more flexible and non-present exteriority of something that is an absolute other of the discourse. The first move signifies ordinary conditions of possibility of repetition. For example, the way phone or verbal signs are produced repetitively marks a fixed relationship between voice and phone. The second move marks the production of an experience by an absolute differentiality of signs. An example of this could be the way voice or phone is written down as an 'outside', or dead marks of living voice/phone as the self-presence of the voice to itself, is dirempted and displaced into marks that have no organic link with voice.[24] So, the case of writing produces a double deal: In its 'literal' sense, it makes the living 'phone' dead, and in its 'figurative' sense, it retains an originary self-presence that the voice contains to itself.

This double sense of 'literal' and 'figural' constitutes the movement of difference in the structure of repetition. The literal determines the totality of signification in language, while the figural determines the possible extension of the field of difference beyond the limits of language. The primordial form of meaning of place and position are neither presence nor sense, but only the form of syntax that intuitively postpones the coming of sense by first bearing a trace of mutual contamination of signs and then extending it beyond the limits of structure to constitute an 'absolute over board'[25] that produces the same when it divides it through multiple iteration and repetition. Therefore, the answer that Derrida gives to the question of effect on the subject or on effect of reproduction of subjectivity turns into (1) an absolute suspension of possibility of objectivity within the self-presence of the subject, and (2) subjectivity falling back upon its ground of difference will constitute itself as an ideal object in itself. The first one shows an originary lack in the constitution of objectivity, while the second one shows that the plenitude or full presence of subject is dependent on an absence of the other.

This simultaneous affectation of a lack and plenitude produces a double bottom of heterogeneity: (1) doubling of the mark inhibiting a total reflective adequation, and (2) a deferral of the mark that prevents the subject forever. Such a double bottom coincides with the double deal of signs in which one cannot choose between living repetition of life and truth and the dead repetition of death and non-truth, because the structure of difference would continually erase the stable position of signs into a reference to the other. This discursive relationship of a fixed determination of the other produces a law of repetition between the signifier and the signified only to repeat and relate them together, because iterability of signifier and signified in the discourse will depend upon identification of self-identical marks. Such identification follows an 'interiorising' of identity inscribed upon a stable 'mark' not subjected to the discursive deferral. One can object here and raise the issue that,

> this interiority belongs to the phenomenological and ideal aspect of every signifier. The ideal form of the written signifier, for example, is not in the world, and the distinction between the grapheme and the empirical body of the corresponding graphic sign separates an inside from outside, phenomenological consciousness from the world.[26]

Derrida would reply to the objection by pointing out that the phenomenological spatial reference lies in the world and this sense of being 'outside' of the world constitutes the phenomenon. But by a strange paradox, meaning is identified through suspension of relation to outside, while expression of meaning in language produces a distance from 'outside' in order to hold meaning in ideal objectivity. Derrida considers such distance from outside as just a representation of the function of language through which representations are validated. This is simultaneously a figurative function of language, which successfully maintains the relationship between the verbal phone and the written sign and by the same forbids the written sign or grapheme in general as an image of the former.[27] It forbids because the written sign links the verbal phone to an exterior, which it delinks in order to retain an ideal objectivity. This blurs the distinction between speech and writing and also redraws the natural relationship between them. Derrida reproduces another account of this relationship:

> Now we must think that writing is at the same time more exterior to speech, not being its 'image' or 'symbol' and more interior to speech, which is already in itself a writing.[28]

Writing as a Generalised Structure of Knowledge

Derrida privileges writing over speech here by upturning the conventional priority of speech over writing. In doing so, he is performing two acts one, a systemic notion of writing that represents the phone, and the other, how representation of the phone in writing divides the writing into two contradictory conventions: (1) writing holding an undecidability between phone and writing and further, (2) in writing, every 'signifier' comes to be treated as a representation or as a metaphor for the signified, assuming that the phone produces graphemes, while every graphic, in its act of signification, can only refer to another standing for a signified. In other words, there is a referral of one signified to another, a displacement of one signified into another through a displacement of one signifier into another. The vertical relationship between signifiers and signified is ungrounded in a plain relationship between signifier and signified.[29] Drawing a parallel again with the interiority of phones, Derrida offers another argument. The interiorisation of writing is a movement from indication to expression and writing becomes a body that expresses something only if we promote the verbal expression that animates it, if its space is temporalised.[30] The temporalised interiority of expression establishes the exteriority of indication so that indication remains outside of expressivity and objectivity. This outside is then expressed and it is further purged into another outside, but expression of all such inside takes its space of voice. In this shelter, temporalised and interiorised space of voice, expression has reduced the outside by bracketing it within. Therefore, the expression is a two-fold 'going forth' of the sense:

> The going forth beyond – itself of an act, then of sense, which can remain in itself, and only in the voice.[31]

The first going forth is the sense through which indication and temporalisation of indication reaches in the interior of voice. This gives a further interiorisation to a space interior to sense in which the sense takes the form of an object. But, this interiorisation of sense into an object opens up the object to an exterior of sense, further opened up to an exterior of expression, later opened up to an exterior of indication. Derrida shows that such simultaneous reversal of exterior into interior and vice versa opens up the possibility of indefinite repetition, the dissimulation of objectivity, sense, meaning and indication as such.[32] But, the irreducibility of the absence of all these as such is an interior repetition, which is a re-call of a sense across a space simultaneously interior and exterior to itself. Such a re-calling produces an inter-subjectivity within the subject even though simultaneous interior and exterior movement of subjectivity produces subject as just an effect of it. But when such a simultaneity is thought of, something that really does this two-fold going forth is the subject that is instituted. Derrida formulates it in these terms:

> The general structure of the unmotivated trace connects within the same possibility and they cannot be separated except by abstraction, the structure of relationship with the other, the movement of temporalisation and language as writing.[33]

So, the insertion of the subject is an institution, which can be viewed as an active synthesis, through the absence of the other, which constitutes the presence, the temporalised exteriority of sense in which it appears as such. The intrusion of an outside, an other into the present produces a dialectic between outside and inside, identity and difference and what the dialectic opens up is an absolute outside in the movement of interiorisation. But, the possibility of reduction of one side of the dialectic to the other lies in the immediate non-self presence of both the sides.[34] The immediate non-self presence is the becoming-space of time in which the exteriority can be interiorised. But, the becoming space of time establishes an interweaving of inside and outside, in which it privileges space as an irreducible outside. Spacing is this interweaving of the relationship between inside and outside, which is neither inside nor outside. If being is presence, if things deserve the application of 'is' in so far as they are present, the spacing is never present, but it is a process of constituting the present, which 'is not' in space, but lies in the becoming space of time. Therefore, spacing is the name for turning inside out of all interiority just as it is a privileging of the outside over inside. The outside, which presents the absence of an other into the exterior of the expression and the non-presence of what lies at the exterior in the expression marks a non-present presence within sense or object in general.[35] Derrida conceptualises it by giving it a new name, *différance*, which is neither a thing nor a concept, but signifies a movement from outside to inside and vice versa within the space of an irreducible difference between signs. This outside of difference names a radical alterity, which is unnameable, yet a possibility of attaining meaning. Derrida describes it in structural terms:

> We could take up all the coupled oppositions on which philosophy is constructed, and from which our language lives, not in order to see opposition vanish, but to see the emergence of a necessity such that one of the terms appear as the difference of the other, the other differed within the systematic ordering of the same (e.g. the intelligible as differing from the sensible, as sensible differed, the concept as differed – differing intuition, life as differed-differing matters, mind as differed – differing life, culture as differed-differing nature (...).[36]

This differed-differing constitutes an interweaving of an inside and outside in the exterior in general represented in the irreducible structure of difference of signs. The simultaneity of differed and differing is temporalised in the form of an ever-present difference in space and ever-present deferral in time, both figuratively signifying a permanent non-presence, an impossibility of reduction of primordial difference. It is not a simple inversion of inside into an outside. It is not a simple inversion of inside into an outside of difference, as such an outside is never available. What is available is a circular and entangled bond between inside and outside through difference. This irreducibility of the structure of difference is conceptualised as the condition of possibility of all significations within language. Differing shall only mean something is different from something else, while deferring shall mean postponement of the completion of an act. The first would signify an ever extending structure in which one sign will differ spatially from the other and the second will signify that the becoming space of time within expression defers the reference of the sign into something absent, which leads to further deferral into something 'past' or 'future'. This is how the sign as a non-present remainder is cut off from what it stands for and its terms of production. Derrida combines this non-present remainder with what it is cut off from in both spatial and temporal mode and gives rise to the neologism 'differance'. The two senses of the terms 'difference' and 'deferment' combine, in the French portmanteau, 'différance'. The term 'differánce' signifies present in absence, while the term deferral signifies a suspension of the 'living present' which is never present. The first one marks the Saussurean implication that signs occupy a place only within a chain of differences, which act as the condition of possibility of signs in general, while deferring is a temporalisation of the exteriority of signs into an interior of expression, sense or speech and the two movements occur simultaneously, resisting the possibility of a unitary signification of expression in a 'unified subject'. Derrida conceptualises this 'differánce' as the double movement of difference and deferral, an intervention into the figuration of difference in space and time and it is this intervention that separates the signifier and the signified in their spatial and temporal presentation. This separation indicates that each differential element in a linguistic system signifies in so far as it refers to another element, and defers its presence to another element and produces a difference with it. Such a character of signs makes it symptomatically related to 'mark' or 'trace' in general, which are reinscribed. What such marks imply is that 'present' or 'experience' in general must refer to something radically other than itself, which is not present and the presence of which is infinitely deferred. Therefore, any attempt of signification would generate such a structure of differential traces, which is constitutive of meaning and meaning in such difference itself:

> It is because of difference that the movement of signification is possible.[37]

This constitutes 'differance' and it makes possible the play of meaning as it is the force behind the reference of one signifier to another. This aspect of difference produces an interval between elements and the temporal relation between elements is 'deferral' and the two together produce a structure which is named achi-writing by Derrida. The production of archi writing is within presence, a writing that produces the structure of difference within presence that produces irreducible archi-syntheses in one and the same possibility of difference producing temporalisation and relationship between signs within language.[38] This relationship assumes the form of a matrix of irreducible oppositions that are produced as an interior and exterior simultaneously. The archi-synthesis always produces a simultaneous 'difference' and 'deferral'. At the level of difference, archi-trace acts as the condition of possibility of metaphysical dyads like presence/absence, time/space and phone/grapheme displacing and interlacing each other. At the level of deferral, the play of opposition between metaphysical dyads produces the becoming spaces of such opposition. For example, the opposition between speech and writing in the moment of deferral will get transformed into the absence of presence. At the moment of difference, speech assumes an interior of writing, which further interiorises speech. But, the archi-synthesis unmakes all the metaphysical opposition into a suspended figure of time or space. What is achieved by archi-synthesis is a positive destruction of 'presence' instituted by philosophy's ethico-theoretic decision to trace its origin as archi-traces or archi-writing that provides a field of non-synonymical substitution. Derrida conceptualises it as 'suspended remains':

> the structural possibility of being weaned from the referent or from the signified seems to me to make every mark (...) a grapheme in general; (...) the non-present *remainder* (resistance) of a differential mark cut off from its positive production or 'origin' and I shall even extend this law to all 'experience' in general if it is conceded that there is no experience consisting of *pure* presence, but only of chains of differential marks.[39]

This extended concept of differential marks constitutes the new science of writing 'grammatology', which does not determine the history of being within the horizon of presence, rather in terms of a determined signifying 'trace'. This field of trace, which implies an originary protowriting from which discourse and language draw their syntax, contains heterogeneous statements not contradictory ones, but of a singular heterogeneity, a field of difference, a negativity homogeneous to all other negatives to resist the general heterogeneity of the whole set of the ontological system. It establishes an exteriority to the heterogeneity by the singularity of difference that resists admission of multiplicity within difference. This makes Derrida wonder what cannot be assimilated in this play of differences, in the space of its possibility. Derrida only prognosticates what cannot be assimilated into the system of difference that supports it from outside and exposes the annulling of the condition that gives rise to the system. This leads to in-assimilable remainders of the system, which cannot be inferred into the 'singular' heterogeneity of the system, which cannot further be interned into general heterogeneity. This binds the statements or concepts, which are able to produce the bond in the system of differences only to bring the decidable statements to undecidable statements in a system of differences. The system of difference, therefore, constricts the movement of traces to 'closing up, squeezing, redressing, subduing, reducing, forcing, subjugating, enslaving, hemming in,[40] an ideality that owes itself to its own inner limits, to this contraction, or this structuration it gives 'itself'. This is the double negation of the negative of difference, first negated into a stable set of rules, further negated into an 'inhibitive construction that recalls both its lack and plenitude, in 'avoiding to lose itself in abstract indetermination', this is a 'displacement', 'counterforce of displacement' or 'condition of relief'. Derrida understands here the relationship between the force of displacement that commits 'violence' to the singularity of difference and cautions against 'strict-ure against stricture' and writes:

> There is no choosing here each time a discourse contre the transcendental is held, a matrix—the (con) striction itself—constrains the discourse to place the non-transcendental, the outside of transcendental field, the excluded in the structuring position. The matrix in question constitutes the excluded as transcendental of the transcendental (...) transcendental contraband. The contraband is *not yet* dialectical contradiction. The contraband remains something other than what necessarily it is to become. Such would be the (non-dialectical) law of the (dialectical) stricture, of the bond (...).[41]

Mapping the Text and the World

What this wants to mean is that differentially ordered signs are not preceded by any meaning, structure or idea; rather, they constitute themselves into an idea that acts as general text to hold the possibility of irreducibility of structure of difference into textuality. Such a generalised structure of text representing the condition of possibility of textuality in general remains extra-textual. It can enforce a stricture and at the same time open the text to the heterogeneity in general. But a 'text' in its relationship with such heterogeneity acquires a definite context on its giving itself to the world. Therefore, 'text' interlaces reference to history, world, reality, being and especially to the other, all those that are not immediately experienced, but experienced as a differentiality. Derrida considers such an experience as 'textual' in the sense that it serves as a framework for accounting for all 'structures' as 'real':

> What I call 'text' implies all the structures called 'real', economic, historical, socio-institutional, in short, all possible referents. Another way of recalling once again that there is nothing outside the text, this does not mean that all referents are suspended, denied (...). But it does not mean that every referent and all reality has the structure of a differential trace (...) and that one cannot refer to this 'real' except in an interpretive experience. The latter neither yields meaning nor assumes it except in a movement of differential referring.[42]

What it means is that the textual representation assumes a differential structure, which means that the reality is never constituted except reciprocally by representation. Within the textual structure of difference, the condition of possibility of representation in the originary absence of what is represented is otherwise presented as an empirical mark. Therefore, Derrida contends:

> One must indeed speak of an originary trace or archi-trace. Yet we know that the concept destroys its name and (...) all beings with trace. There is above all no originary trace.[43]

It is in the space of archi-traces brought inside the horizon of presence that deconstruction takes place in the form of taking into account the limitless context. It is here upon the surface of a context that deconstruction takes place in the form of textualisation, as an affirmative move and, simultaneously, it proceeds through the text to uncover the lines of forces that order the trace structure within the text. Within the text, spacing of the traces is the 'becoming-absent' and 'becoming-unconscious' of the subject. The signification is formed within this hollow of difference between what is appearing in the text and the appearance. Derrida characterises this difference as a 'non-fundamental structure':

> In such a structure (....) at once superficial and bottomless (...) the property is literally sunk (....) it passes into the other.[44]

This non-fundamental structure of text transforms the hierarchical structure between reality and representation and reverses it into its opposites. Production of such a structure of reversal is meant for instituting the difference into the text. By institution of such difference, the text draws its closure around it in its relationship with what it means to say. Difference is thereby subsumed under meaning. This subsumption of meaning under difference does not enable a text to construct a meaning wholly, but constructs it partially by taking resort to an ideality that marks a transition from phenomenon to its condition of possibility. But this resorting to transcendental conditions of possibility is the return of a moment of unconditional activity forgotten in the construction of a text. Remembering the unconditionality is an irreducible opening of the text beyond its 'closure', but this in itself does not free the text from subsumption under the laws of production to which it shows its never inextinguishable fidelity. Derrida contends that structure of difference also accounts for this fidelity by giving it an ontological status in terms of belonging to the 'law'. What Derrida intends is to remove the fidelity of the structure of difference to the law of abstraction of the text by way of referring to the unconditional as well as to the conditions of possibility, none of which are present within the text. The double reference to unconditional (difference) and the condition of possibility (of knowledge) only issue from a text, instead of constructing the text themselves. Derrida argues that context articulates the conditions of possibility for experience in general and the context itself is conditioned by the unconditioned, by that which is independent of 'a context in general'. Derrida argues that such an 'unconditioned', arises as the interruption and non-closure of any determined context. It is an injunction that 'transcends' all contexts. Such an unconditioned paradoxically acts as the condition of possibility of texts in general and conditions it through differences that point to a differential matrix of generation of names and concepts produced as its effect:

> The unnameable is not an ineffable being which no name can approach: God, for example. This unnameable is the play which makes possible nominal effects, the relatively unitary and atomic structures that are called names, the chains of substitutions of names in which, for example, the nominal effect difference is itself enmeshed.[45]

The eruption of the unconditional within the conditioned is an unnameable difference signifying only a 'dynamic' which can neither be re-called as nostalgia nor be prognosticated as the ultimate, which is 'never be' or 'never is', but an absolute alterity which is never present, but just an 'indication':

> It governs nothing, reigns over nothing, and nowhere exercises any authority, it is not announced by any capital letter. Not only is there no kingdom of difference, but difference instigates the subversion of every kingdom. Which makes it obviously threatening and infallibly dreaded by everything within us that desires a kingdom, the past or future presence of a kingdom.[46]

Such an absolute alterity, which marks the possibility of the exit of alterity outside of itself and of signification in so far as it is constituted by reduction of difference into a fixed meaning of the entity. Such a fixed meaning of the entity in hierarchical or differential terms ground their iterability in the outside of itself. Construction of the unconditional as space, which is again the context in general, makes possible the illegibility of the concepts by giving it an exit. Such an exit is described by

Derrida as a 'we must affirm this', and say yes to the unnameable that acts as the injunction to affirm the unconditioned and it produces deconstruction:

> The yes, which says nothing, describes nothing but itself, the performance of its own event of affirmation repeats itself, quotes, cites itself, says yes to itself as (to an) other in accordance with the ring (......).[47]

Deconstruction here produces two steps: the step beyond the presence, the irrevocable being or non-being of something finished, and across inert events. This exposes present to what is coming, a displacement that indicates an irreducible alterity, and the 'not beyond', no going beyond, to make possible the coming of the other. This means deconstruction is not wholly transgressive of what is conditioned as a text, but it repeats the possibility of the text by taking a step beyond. Derrida expresses such a state of being within and without as a 'horizon of waiting', which acts as a phase of 'stepping beyond' and a phase of displacement or re-citation of what is already there. Derrida calls it a 'double gesture':

> We must proceed using a double gesture, according to a unity that is both systematic and in and of itself divided (......).[48]

The phase of stepping beyond indicates the irreducible alterity within the system and re-citation is constituted by this alterity, an invention of the same in a newer form. Deconstruction is inventive, or it does not exist.[49] When the first gesture takes place, it is entirely within the unity of the system, 'across or inert event' constitutes the step beyond, that is a move away from the gross; the second gesture breaks through the unity and re-inscribes what is invested by taking the step beyond. Deconstruction is engaged in and by the incoming, the arrival of what is coming, and it makes possible what to come in and by the future and the adventure of the future,[50] the advent of future from the abyss that stems out of the unity of the system or the conventions. Deconstruction, therefore, produces a trespassable margin between what exists and what is to come, an unnameable mark separating the presence and the future. It produces invisibility between the two phases turned onto one another, a simulacrum of the present and the future in the invisibility between the two phases. Being within the present, the visibility of the present depends upon a certain bind of the present manifested in a specularity conditioned by differential in-appearance of the present as trace is something like 'X without the X', the unknown without itself. This is what Derrida also characterised as 'conjuration', which leads one to draw an apparition or a line between 'what is there' and what is 'there to come' and hit upon the 'specular' or the 'apparition', a bodyless body, a kind of 'body without property'. Derrida says:

> The constative form tends to reassure.
> The certification is effective (...).
> it is effectively performative.[51]

Derrida considers this reassurance of the 'performative' as ensuring that philosophy is a 'philosophy of ontology', where the alterity of the other assumes a specular form or gives it a certitude to the visible interior of the text. Within this certitude, there is no question of opposing the invention of same to the invention of other, which is different differently,

> (...) difference beckons towards another coming about, toward this other invention of which we dream, the invention of the wholly other, the one that allows the coming of a still unanticipatable alterity, and for which no horizon of waiting as yet seems ready, in place, available.[52]

Deconstruction as Critique and Critique as Deconstruction

Divested of even a 'horizon of waiting' within the textuality of the constative, one must still prepone for it. Like a heroic subjective agent, we must prepare ourselves to invent the wholly other: 'to prepare oneself for this coming (venue) of the other is what can be called deconstruction'.[53] One can say that deconstruction directs itself towards the wholly other, the impossible, the dream of what is not and which does not belong within the horizon of what presently prevails. Once again, a 'double gesture', a criss-crossing between what is there and what is yet to come, this experience is characterised by Derrida:

> (...)to invent would then be to "know how to say 'come' and to answer the 'come' of the other. Does that ever come about? Of this event, one is never sure.[54]

But this saying 'come' signifies a state of knowledge that does not follow the already existing discourse, but treats through it; it is constituted and dislocated at the same time. Therefore:

> (...) the question 'what is' belongs to a space (ontology and from it the knowledge of grammar, linguistics, semantics and so on) opened by a 'come' come from the other.[55]

This sense of 'come' cannot become an object, theme or representation, but an opening which can only be demonstrated in language such that it remains as the other of language that comes in the 'step beyond' and 'not beyond' language. This 'other' manifests in the irreducible structure of difference that language houses in:

> constituting and dislocating it at the same time, writing is other than the subject, in whatever sense the latter is understood. Writing can never be thought under the category of the subject, however it is modified, however it is endowed with consciousness or unconsciousness, it will refer by the entire thread of its history, to a substantiality of a presence unperturbed by accidents, or to the identity of the self-same proper in the presence of self-relationship.[56]

Manifestation of the 'other' in writing continuously dislocates any reference to the self and hence any movement of idealisation in the text will inherently be fractured between 'self' and the 'other' in a perpetual absence of the both. Such a fracture appears as a kind of 'fork', one of the sides extended further than the other in such a way that when the 'self' posits an 'other', the 'other' never comes and the self remains in a perpetual state of waiting, preparing itself for the other. This keeps the discourse open-ended:

> Would it not at once cease to be the other? Would the event have arrived yet? Would it not be struck by its interdiction (...) by its very arrival?[57]

This question puts the 'other' under 'erasure'. In the textual structuring of the conceptual oppositions, no concept can itself remain metaphysical; it has to efface itself in order to refer to the other. This erasure is the possibility of becoming of concepts within a frame of convention and rules. Therefore, deconstruction invents the permissible and the possible, which is the inventiveness of a 'human subject',[58] invention in conformity with already established conventions. Two consequences follow from these: one, bending such conventions, in order to allow the other to come in the opening of such conventions, and second, invention invents nothing new. Both these consequences follow because:

> nothing comes to the other or from the other. For the other is not the possible. So it would be necessary to say that the only possible invention is the invention of the impossible (...).[59]

This is how deconstruction gets embroiled in a paradox of the impossible, which sets it in motion, by means of which deconstruction can let it come:

> I am careful to say 'let it come' because if the other is precisely what is not invented, the initiative or deconstructive inventiveness can consist only in the opening, in unclosetting, destabilising foreclusionary structures so far as to allow for the passage toward the other. But one does not make the other come, one lets it come by preparing for its coming.[60]

Play of Presence and Absence

This perpetual non-presence of the other in the inventiveness of the other takes it outside the textual fabric within which deconstruction operates. The name or concept of something disappears in the shrouds of otherness, which permanently delay the wholly other. Derrida says:

> There is no such thing as a 'metaphysical concept'. There is no such thing as a 'metaphysical name'. The metaphysical is a certain determination or direction taken by a chain, one cannot oppose it to a concept, but to a process of textual labour and another enchaining.[61]

The concept tends to disappear to efface itself, to make itself meaningless in the process of enchaining. It becomes a 'name sans name'. It does so precisely to point to the possibility of the wholly other which never falls into presence. Deconstruction obeys strange syntax of the 'sans':

> The same word and the same thing appear removed from themselves, substracted from their reference and from their identity, fully continuous with letting themselves be traversed, in their old body, towards a 'wholly other' dissimulated in them. But no more than in *pas* does this consist in a simple privation or negation, far from it (...). It forms the trace or the step (*pas*) of the *tout autre* that is at issue in it, the re-treat of the *pas*, and of the *pas sans pas*.[62]

Such a re-inscription is an act of circumscribing and circumventing the invention of something within the discourse, which carries the tradition or convention. Derrida puts it under the erasure of 'promise'.

> I will speak of a promise, then, but also within the promise.[63]

The point here is to remain active in placing oneself within the commitment of meaning and being, but as soon as one re-inscribes such a commitment within promise, there is 'never present commitment arising prior to commitment', the promise is already stripped away. But such stripping away is the source of the injunction that produces an unconditional moment of affirmation. This stripping away is simultaneously a 'sending' and a 'returning', which is beyond the closure of representation. Both sending and returning are unconditioned, as they lie beyond every determinate context or beyond determination of context in general, that is it marks an absence of an addressee to whom the promise of sending is made and to whom returns the promise. So, writes:

> Following this, what remains is to articulate this unconditionally with the determinate conditions of this or that context (...). The structure thus described supposes that there are only contexts, that nothing exists outside context (...) the limit of the frame or the border of the context always entails as closure of non-closure(...).The outside penetrates and thus determines the inside.[64]

Deconstructing Reason

Therefore, thinking of an exteriority as the other of the discourse problematises the exteriority as well as the boundary of the discourse. An analoguous case of experience is the self-identical identification of such a subject that involves identification of how it is constituted, the basis of its presence lies in its self-identical action, role and continuity. Derrida, by questioning the notion of a proper other, questions the representation of such an other as subject or as a subject's relation-to-its-other, because such a subject always remains an other to itself by erasing itself in any act of signification. The history of the subject as constructed in western metaphysics accords it a place only through an 'effect of anterior absence and temporalisation'. Prior to all cognition and memory, the subject is a 'trace', wandering through its presence, which is never self-present. After the acts of cognition and memory, this wandering trace gets engaged in a network of consciousness filled up with a system of signifiers that constantly defects to various fields of signification. In this kind of situation of difference, the subject appears only as an effect of centring or closure of the discourse that cannot be conceptualised on the basis of presence. But it remains as a discourse instituted as an exchange with an exterior, a trace:

> prior to every proposition and even before all discourse in general (...) preserves a trace of the other. A trace of an even older than it or a 'taking place' to come, both of them: here there is neither an alternative nor a contradiction.[65]

This trace enters into a relation of erasing one other, which is a series of interruptions, which leave its traces of erasure as an encounter with the other. But this entails a moment of affirmation of the other through which the subject can be constituted and, therefore, deconstruction or erasure becomes a positive response to an alterity which necessarily calls, summons or motivates it. Such is an alterity that institutes an other to precede philosophy to give rise to a rapport, through which the subject can express itself. Again such a rapport is answering to the call of together which opens up the limits of signification that act as a 'transcendental contract' that 'renders possible every 'contract'. Such a possibility makes a text able to answer to what Derrida calls the call of reason. The principle of reason always demands an answer by rendering these principles on their 'grounds' that are conserved in a discourse of reason. Derrida says:

> To respond to the call of reason is to 'render reason', to explain effects through their causes, rationally; it is also to ground, to justify, account for on the basis of principle of roots.[66]

But answering the call of reason is to question the grounds of reason and to ask questions like, "Are we to use reason to account for the principle of reason? Is the reason for reason rational?" The questions imply certain annihilation of reason by asking ground for reason, if there are grounds at all. But the question of ground of reason 'annihilates' annihilation of reason, as reason is already formed without a ground, without a self-sufficient principle and so asking a question about the ground of reason demarcates the reason for asking the question and 'what is asked for' in order to open up our questioning of grounds of reason and our acts of giving reasons. Deconstruction, therefore, opens up a dialogue between abyssal structure and what the structure represents. Derrida characterised it thus:

> Are we obeying the principle of reason when we ask what grounds this principle, which is itself a principle of grounding? We are not, which does not mean that we are disobeying it either, are we dealing here with a circle or with an abyss? The circle would consist in seeking to account for reason by reason, to render reason to the principle of reason, in appealing to the principle in order to make it speak of itself at the very point where (....). (...)the principle of reason says nothing about itself. The abyss (...) would be the impossibility for a principle of grounding to ground itself (...) Who is more faithful to reason's call, who hears it with a keener ear who better sees the deference, the one who offers questions in return and tries to think through the possibility of that summons, or the one who does not to want to hear about the reason of reason?[67]

The double bottomlessness of having no ground to ground the principle of reason as well as un-grounding reason by questioning its grounds produces a breach between principle and discourse and discourse and its ground realised in the methodological operation of deconstruction. It recognises an irreducible non-presence, recognises as a constitutive value, which brings in 'an ineradicable non-originarity' to any act of self-reflexivity or claim of subjecthood.

These deconstructed interiors of the field of difference acts as a condition of possibility for a simultaneous reinscription of the components of a discourse, which is 'derivable' from the destructuring of a field of discourse. At this level, the de-structured elements of a hierarchy assume a singularity as a primal affirmation, which is also absolutely divisible. Such a singularity within a deconstructed discourse requires repetition with alternation and the alternation produces citation. This citation is an affirmation of itself, which would be deciphered. But the citation is expressed and the moment it is expressed, it is a response to a solicitation of the other, beyond-being. This logic of citation is not governed here by any appropriation, but it is just a giving itself to the other. But this giving itself becomes another appropriation if it is determined already by an interpretative discourse. Still, it is a drift headed to the wholly other 'underivable from the identity of a determination'. It is just this undeterminable drift through which the giving can prolong its addresses without message and without destination, without sender or decidable address. This produces a strange syntax of de-construction in which the citation is 'X sans X'; it is not a simple negation, multiplication or destruction, but a certain reinscription of X, a certain reversal of the movement of X that still communicates with X. This communication is something like disruption of all symmetry between the conscious 'self' and its portrait, a non-identity with itself. This non-identity 'folds' into a 'double bind' between the non-self identity and the self in which self resembles the non-self identity by becoming 'non-self'. This is how a fold produces a response to the non-self-identical which is a deconstructive 'yes', a certain trembling that comes back to itself with the trace of the other, which remains as an outside to the yes. But what yes is this? This yes refers back to itself, comes back to itself, 'reference of itself to itself which at the same time never leaves itself and never happens to arrive'. This is where we have finally abandoned the play of reference.[68]

In Lieu of Conclusion

To sum up, the very activity of thinking, which too happens on the basis of epistemological, ontological and veridical comprehension, is the reduction of plurality into unity and alterity into sameness. Philosophy in the western tradition has been aiming at the most to grasp and to domesticate the other and so the goal of Derrida's deconstruction is not simply to recover the unthought of tradition, but to understand that-which-cannot be-thought; it is to point towards that which philosophy is unable to say. Deconstruction attempts to locate 'a non-site, or a non-philosophical site, from which to question philosophy'. But to reach such a site, paradoxically, deconstruction has to draw its resources from within the tradition of philosophy or logocentrism. Deconstruction assumes a 'double bind' of both belonging to a philosophical system, which at the same time is not capable of belonging to the system. This becomes possible because deconstruction unravels the condition of possibility of a text by belonging to it and at the same time opens the text up to the unconditional exterior by interrogating/defying those conditions of possibility.

The irreducible opening of a text to the unconditional lies beyond every determinate context, even of the determination of context in general. The unconditional not only announces its presence in the opening of the text, it intervenes in the construction of a text from its very opening and forms a law that transcends the very determination of this context and context in general. The unconditionality needs to be articulated by way of opening the conditioned context to the indeterminable context of responsibility and this is how it is opened to the conditioned indetermination. The conditioned context is deferred in the moment of opening up the conditioned and the unconditioned context conditions it in different ways producing difference in the determined context. The unconditioned context affirms with a determination and the moment of affirmation bears an injunction that entails a non-closure in the text.

Such an unconditioned context is opened up in the very idea of sign that represents the present in its absence. The sign institutes an auto-affection linked up with an irreducible non-presence that has a contributive role. The contribution of the sign is marked by the effacement of voice and by its difference from other elements in language. This negative non-presence in sign links it up with a science of writing that deals with the auto-affection among signs in a chain.

That knowledge ideally requires unconditioned justification can only be mediated through the auto-affection of signs, which generates concepts or ideas, reinscribed back in the non-reflexive and non-present exteriority of the absolute other.

Derrida's reading of Marx's *Capital* in terms of an already inscribed time that terminates circulation in order to produce value that assumes the 'form' of human relationship, the 'form' which gives rise to specular entity, a phenomenon marked 'X' for any phenomenological perception. Similarly, Derrida's affirmation that by thinking of the other as the proper margin, philosophy is never surprised by its outside in the extreme 'elitism' of subject-centred reason.

Notes

1. Jacques Derrida, *Margins of Philosophy*, trans. Alan Bass, University of Chicago Press, Chicago, 1982, p. 172. Henceforth, *MP*.
2. Jacques Derrida, *Speech and Phenomena and other Essays on Husserl's Theory of Signs,* trans. David Allison, Northwestern University Press, Evanston, 1973, p. 133. Henceforth, *SP*.
3. Jacques Derrida, *L'Archeologie du Frivole*, Lire Cadillace, Denel/Gothier, Paris, 1976, p. 14. Henceforth, *AF*.
4. Jacques Derrida, *Positions*, trans. Alan Bass, University of Chicago Press, Chicago, p. 82. Henceforth *P*.
5. Jacques Derrida,, *Writing and Difference,* trans. Alan Bass, University of Chicago Press, Chicago, 1978, p. 279. Henceforth, *WD*.
6. *WD*, pp. 280-281.

7. *MP*, p. 172, p. 77.
8. Jacques Derrida, *Word Traces: Readings of Paul Celan,* ed. A. Fioretos, John Hopkins University Press, Baltimore, 1994, p. 68. Henceforth, *WT.*
9. *SP*, p. 5.
10. *SP*, p. 53.
11. *SP*, p. 62.
12. *WT*, p. 68.
13. *SP*, p. 57.
14. Jacques Derrida,, *Dissemination*, trans. Barbara Johnson, University of Chicago Press, Chicago, 1981, p. 223. Henceforth, *D.*
15. *D*, p 256.
16. Jacques Derrida, *Spurs: Nietzsche's Styles*, trans. Barbara Harlow, University of Chicago Press, Chicago, 1978, p. 177. Henceforth, *S.*
17. "A Discussion with Jacques Derrida", *Writing Instructor*, Vol. 9, No. 1-2 p. 15.
18. *SP*, p. 50.
19. *MP*, p. 121.
20. *MP*, p. 13.
21. *P*, p. 71.
22. *SP*, pp. 85-86.
23. *MP*, p.21.
24. Jacques Derrida, *Of Grammatology*, trans. Gayatri Chakrabarty Spivak, John Hopkins University Press, Baltimore, 1976, p. 29. Henceforth, *OG.*
25. *OG*, p. 154.
26. *SP*, p. 85/86.
27. *OG*, p. 45.
28. *OG*, p. 46.
29. *MP*, pp. 260-1.
30. *MP*, p, 91.
31. *SP*, p. 35.
32. *OG*, p. 47.
33. *OG*, p. 47.
34. *SP*, p. 40.
35. *SP*, p. 40.
36. *MP* pp. 18-19.
37. *MP*, p. 13.
38. Jacques Derrida, *Limited Inc.*, trans. Samuel Weber, Northwestern University Press, Evanston, 1988, p. 10. Henceforth, *LI.*

39. Jacques Derrida, *Glas*, trans. John P. Leavy Jr. and Richard Rand; University of Nebraska Press, Lincoln, 1986, p. 94. Henceforth, *G*.
40. *G*, p. 107.
41. *G*, p, 244.
42. *LI*, p. 148.
43. *OG*, p. 61.
44. *S*, p. 117.
45. *S*, p. 81.
46. *MP*, p 22.
47. Jacques Derrida, "Living On/Borderlines", trans. James Hulber, in Harold Bloom et al, *Deconstruction and Criticism*, New York, Continuum, 1979, p. 104. Henceforth *LO*.
48. *P*, p. 41.
49. Jacques Derrida, *Reading de Man Reading*, ed. Lindsay Waters and Wlad Godzich, University of Minnesota Press, Minneapolis, 1989, p. 43. Henceforth, *RDR*.
50. Jacques Derrida, *Points ...... Interviews*, 1974-94, ed. Elisabeth Weber, trans. Peggy Kamuf et al., Stanford University Press, Stanford, 1995, p. 127. Henceforth, *Point.*
51. Jacques Derrida, *Spectre of Marx,* trans. Peggy Kamuf, Routledge, New York, 1994, p. 48. Henceforth, *SM.*
52. *RDR*, p. 55.
53. Jacques Derrida, *The Other Heading: Reflections on Today's Europe,* trans. P.A. Brault et al, Indiana University Press, Bloomington, 1992.
54. *RDR*, p. 52.
55. Jacques Derrida, *Raising the Tone of Philosophy, Late Essays by Immanuel Kant, Transformative Critique by Jacques Derrida,* ed. Peter Fenves, John Hopkins University Press, Baltimore, 1993, p. 166. Henceforth, *RTP.*
56. *OG.*, pp. 68-9.
57. Jacques Derrida, *Parages*, Galilee, Paris, 1986, p. 66. Henceforth, *Parages*.
58. *RDR*, p. 60.
59. *RDR*, p. 60.
60. *RDR*, p. 60.
61. *D*, p.6.
62. *Parages*, p. 90.
63. *Derrida and Negative Theology*, ed. H. Coward and T. Foshay, SUNY Press, Albany, 1992, p. 84. Henceforth, *DNT.*
64. *LI*, pp. 152-3.

65. Jacques Derrida, "How to Avoid Speaking" in *Language of the Unsayable*, (ed.), S. Budick and W. Iser, Columbia University Press, New York, pp. 3-70, see p. 20.
66. Jacques Derrida, "The Principle of Reason", *Diacritics,* Fall 1983, pp. 3-20, see p. 8. Henceforth, *PR*.
67. *PR*, p. 9.
68. Jacques Derrida, "Archive Fever: A Freudian Impression", trans. Eric Perenowitz, *Diacritics* 25 (1995), pp. 9-63, p. 45.

IV

Postmetaphysical Critique of Knowledge

Habermas' Project of Modernity

Postmetaphysical Critique and Theory of Knowledge: A Simultaneous Intervention

Habermas aims at pursuing the normative dimensions of modernity[1] minus its ontological-metaphysical 'grounds', which for him are already realised in the very structure of normative principles.[2] Such a normative dimension stems from the existing rules and norms governing individual and collective action in various forms of societies streamlined further in well-defined spheres of life.[3] Habermas makes a distinction between the rules and norms guiding the actions of members of societies and the functional rules guiding the operation of various spheres of life with an increasingly differentiated network of subsystems. This distinction is based upon Habermas' categorical distinction between 'life-world' and 'system' in which the former relates to culturally, traditionally and conventionally structured norms and values that regulate the relationship between the individual and the world; while the latter means the structuring of society in functionally coordinated and autonomous organisations that reproduce society in the complex system.[4] Habermas distinguishes the two in normative terms as well: The former strictly bases itself upon pre-interpreted and mutually shared norms and values differentiating various spheres of life, while the latter bases itself upon an objectivated media-steered process mechanism of functioning independent of values and norms. Therefore, at one level, Habermas gives life-world a foundational basis, while at another level, he uncouples it to give 'system' a foundational basis. Life-world links it up with the 'forms of rationalisation'[5] that created differentiated spheres and their corresponding subsystems.

In rethinking critical theory, Habermas highlights these forms of rationalisation[6], which derive their essentials from life-world mores and can reproduce the life-world in the coordination of various actions and spheres of life. This reproduction of life-world norms is possible only through linguistically mediated communication between actors. Habermas emphasises the indispensability of linguistic mediation as it is the only medium that can coordinate all the three spheres of life, namely objective, subjective and intersubjective, through propagation of reasons that emerge specifically for each of the spheres.[7] Along with these spheres, the emergence of a de-liguistified steering media that coordinates various subsystems namely money and power, stabilises the unintended interconnections of mores. In the case of linguistic mediation, communication takes place through securing normative aspects, and in the case of media, communication takes place through technical integration of various subsystems.[8] Corresponding to this dual realm of life-world and system, Habermas claims an overlapping of the two in the reproduction of the 'inner logic' of the symbolic structures of the life world and the systemic maintenance of its material substratum. But this reproduction cannot influence the functioning of subsystems and, as a result, it suppresses forms of social integration in areas where reproduction of life world norms brings about 'a consensus dependent coordination of action'.[9] This brings about a situation when mediatisation of the life-world assumes the form of a colonisation. So, in the ultimate analysis, the logic of the system subsumes the normative sphere of the life-world. Paradoxically, Habermas thinks of a rationalisation process which reproduces the value sphere of the life-world only to be subsumed under the technicalised coordinating mechanism of the system. This is derived from two mutually disparate positions: one, that of Kant dividing human reason into spheres of pure, practical and aesthetic that synchronise with Weber's theory of social differentiation[10] and the other, the Parsonian subsumption of rationalisation of the life-world under the growth of system complexity. It leads to an assimilation of rationalisation of the life-world to the processes of system differentiation. This assimilation bears two consequences: one, the growing autonomy of society in relation to the rationalisation of the life-world, and two, increasing system complexity marking greater rational shaping of the conditions of life. The process of assimilation merges the rationalisation processes of the life-world into the complexity of the system. What Habermas derives from this mode of assimilation is a conceptual harmonisation of the rationalised life-world with the increasing complexity of the social system. The harmonisation produces a parallel synchrony between spheres of life, validity claims and differentiation of the system with respect to the Kantian tripartition of reason into scientific, moral and aesthetic categories. Validity claims assume three types, true, legitimate and authentic, with their correlates in truth, goodness and beauty, all of which jibe with their correspondence to systemic differentiation of subsystems like society, culture and personality. What Habermas does here is to delineate these differentiated spheres and mark their integration in terms of an ontological grounding of 'interaction' between human beings and the world in three-fold pragmatic relations obtainable between them:

(1) to something in the objective world (as the totality of entities about which true statements are possible);

(2) to something in the social world (as the totality of legitimately regulated interpersonal relations), and
(3) to something in the subjective world (as the totality of experiences to which one as speaker has privileged access and which she can express in public).[11]

An Integrated Theory of Modernity

These relationships, Habermas contends, turn up in pure types of action oriented to 'mutual understanding', which follows out of the speech acts to each kind of relationship grounded in the life-world context of society.

In the case of assimilation of life-world rationalisation within systemic integration, Habermas integrates these three modes of relationships in one theory, which, for him, is also a theory of 'modernity'. The question that is addressed in such a theory is, "What is the medium of integration of the life-world and system?" Habermas' answer to this question follows from the role played by language in everyday communication. The role played by language is determined by the normative function that it performs between the life-world and system by embedding integration in the formal principles of systemic coordination. But the question arises, how can an embedding of the normative values and conventions of the life-world in language serve to coordinate the various subsystems of societal organisation? For example, how can language integrate subsystems like economic production and law in one system? The life-world orientation to action as contained in language in the form of norms, values and facts cannot be immediately transferred to technical sites of production or procedural aspects of legality as the life-world and system do not share a common code of norms and values. If the transfer takes place from the life-world to the system and vice versa, does it happen in the way rationalisation of the life-world is regulated by technicalisation of the system? Habermas produces a theory of communicative action that eliminates this greater influence of the system upon the life-world by way of a set of universal pragmatic rules followed in communication without a distinction between the life-world and the system. The overwhelming reason given by Habermas is his notion of 'contexts of relevance'[12], articulated in language in terms of themes and goals of action in a life-world situation and in terms of 'steering media'[13] available in the system technicising[14] the life-world. The language can embed both the context and the media in the forms of rationalisation involved in both these connectives and conjunctives. The form of rationalisation produces a distinction between context and media, and language can differently articulate the functional aspects of both these. Habermas describes the two cases differently:

> (1) A situation is a segment of life-world contexts of relevance (...) by themes and articulated through goals and plans of action; these contexts of relevance are concentrically ordered and become increasingly anonymous and diffused as the spatiotemporal and social distance grows,[15]

> (2) Steering media such as money and power (...) encode purposive rational dealings with calculable amounts of value and make it possible to exert generalised strategic influence (...) because they not only simplify communication on language, but replace it with a symbolic generalisation of negative and positive sanctions, the life-world context in which processes of reaching understanding always remain embedded gets devalued. The life-world is no longer necessary for coordinating actions.[16]

These two characterisations of the role of language demonstrate that these kinds of rational action determine the communicative function of language even though the three-fold possible modes of actor-world relationship in the life-world is structurally retained within language. What determines communication is the specification of roles to be played by language and, thereby, the coordination enacted by language between the life-world and the system gets influenced by such role-deciding sources. The situation develops into a two-fold critique of rationalisation One, it undercuts the relevance of the life-world, and two, it gives rise to a breach or fragmentation between the life-world and the system thematised by Habermas in his notion of 'internal colonisation' of the life-world, meaning 'rationality of knowing and acting subjects (....), systematically expand into a purposive rationality of a higher order'.[17] This is further explained in terms of the life-world, 'rationality of self-regulating systems, whose imperatives outside the consciousness of the members integrated into them, appears in the shape of a totalised purposive rationality'.[18]

These two 'folds' of critique turn into a generalised critique of rationalisation in which Habermas distinguishes two forms, one the instrumental rationality oriented to success, and the other, the emancipatory rationality oriented to undistorted communication. What he terms as instrumental rationality as a form of rationalisation justifies the functioning of the system, while emancipatory rationality comes through the strategic interests involved in the functioning of the system in favour of life-world orientation to reach mutual understanding. Habermas puts the language of the life-world norms as 'encoded' in its pragmatic uses. It becomes emancipatory in the sense that it overcomes the limited, goal-oriented and strategic use of language and recovers/retrieves the life-world norm from under the colonised subsystems of life. Such retrieval also removes the possibility of a backward return to traditions that contains the rationalisation of a differentiated life-world along with an elimination of these systemic rules that purport to finish off life-world norms. The way Habermas does it acquires an ontological-epistemological foundation. Opposed to the systemic coordination of the three-fold possibilities of a relationship between the action and the world to prerogatives of integration, the emancipatory form of rationlisation produces and integrates an ontological-epistemological foundation. This systemic integration involves all three components of the 'actor-world' relationship, namely objective, subjective and intersubjective, in a symbiosis in which none of them can ensure communication in an independent manner. In other words, the essential epistemological-ontological condition for something to be objectively true is to become intersubjectively legitimate and subjectively authentic simultaneously, breach of which would make it a strategic perspective serving only a purposive end. The important question here is to see how the three folds get enmeshed into one another and which mode of rationalisation makes this possible.

Habermas' line of argument here is two-fold: one, making those claims valid which are objectively true, socially legitimate and expressive of authenticity of its incumbents, and two, reconstruction of the life-world and third systemic norms are based upon this integrated perspective. A combination of the three folds makes a claim stand on a different reason than the traditional metaphysical, epistemological or ontological basis. It stands upon a new criterion of integrated perspective. This is what make it specifically oriented to communication and Habermas relates it to post-Kantian developments for philosophy. A combination of the three staves off the possibility of a fragmented, partial and context-based claim of truth. Habermas locates this possibility in the functioning of modern social systems in which an integration of the life-world norms with systemic imperative makes possible a critique of these theories of knowledge in the western tradition which justifies partial truth claims mostly based upon a metaphysical conception of reality. In the tune of reconstruction of these norms and values that arise out of the life-world through the process of rationalisation in the system, Habermas advances an alternative brand of philosophical theories that takes into account the direct role of language in coordination of actions specific to differentiated spheres of the life-world and system. Habermas proposes a non-phenomenological and non-metaphysical notion of the life-world contra-Husserl in which removal of the subject would enable one to see language as a repository of the most fundamental relationships with the world, where 'world' also stands out without being reduced to 'noema'. Extending this argument, Habermas proposes to construct phenomena in terms of intersubjectively regulated and agreed upon norms of action. This tendency of neutralising the subject leads Habermas to consider language as a repository of formal principles of the life-world minus its roots in culture and tradition. Further, the divergences between world-views that constrain mutual intersubjective understanding between cultures is removed by Habermas by reconstructing certain common value-neutral and universalisable criteria of linguistic communication that transcend the specific grammatical, syntactical and other rules of language. Rather, languages are reinterpreted in terms of their action coordinating potential by way of creating a set of rules that act in common between cultures only to serve the purpose of mutual exchange and knowledge of each other.

Therefore, Habermas' basic project of critique of instrumental rationality by exploring the communicative dimension of language takes a transcultural and transcontextual turn coinciding with theories of language and its uses as advocated by contemporary analytical and European philosophers. Secondly, it gives rise to a unified theory of modernity.

Knowledge as a 'Disinterested' and 'Emancipatory' Pursuit

It is necessary here to revisit Habermas' recreation of theory of communication through integration of various claims of knowledge and truth stemming out in three folds of relationship with the world. Habermas theorises these three folds of relationship in terms of knowledge constitutive interests. These are also three-fold: (1) the technical/instrumental interest of empirical analytic sciences, (2) the practical/ethical interest of hermeneutic science, and (3) the emancipatory/communicative interest of the critical sciences. As we have discussed earlier, the emancipatory interest of the communicative action is what gives it the necessary basis for integrating the three folds of relationship with the world and it also provides the fulcrum for critique of the instrumental character of rationality embedded in the breached processes of communication in the subordinated integration of the life-world within the systematic totalisation. Therefore, a brief discussion of all the knowledge constitutive interests would enable us to bring out the emancipatory potential of critical sciences in terms of communicative action and establish their critical edge over other such interests.

Habermas finds that the object domain of science is represented in the statement of facts consisting of strictly methodological correlatives. Metatheoretical reflections of science strengthen such methodological correlatives in terms of action aimed at 'control of external conditions of existence' and activities as controlled observation, experimentation and measurement only furnish cases of success or failures of operation. Habermas states:

> In the empirical-analytical sciences, the frame of reference that prejudges the meaning of possible statements establishes rules both for the construction of theories and for theoretical testing. Theories comprise hypothetical deductive connections of prepositions, which permit the deduction of law like hypotheses with empirical content. The latter can be interpreted as statements about the covariance of observable events; given a set of initial conditions, they make predictions possible (...). However, the meaning of such propositions, that is their technical exploitability, is established only by the rules according to which we apply theories of reality.[19]

This kind of rationality of science reduces reality into some theoretical entities that express an objective relationship. Such an expression only uses language in an instrumental sense as it is directed towards a relationship between the human subject and the object as if it were a relationship between object and object. As opposed to such reduction to the object-object relationship in a subject-independent idea of 'reality', the communicative rationality establishes relationships in all three possible dimensions, which is a move beyond the already settled relationships between individual and world.

Contrastingly, historical-hermeneutic science has as its object the nature of human language and interaction, that is symbolic and communicative expressions that produce intersubjective meaning. This itself became the mode of self-understanding of the actors in terms of norms through which they relate mutually to each other. As an implication, hermeneutic science has to deal with the conditions of possibility of reaching mutual agreement which leads to a common praxis for various communities. In other words, hermeneutic science establishes the relationship between self-understanding and the existing practices to serve the practical interest of the group or community as a whole. Based on such self-understanding, an authentic ethical perspective on life could be constructed so that integration of mutual understanding and practical application is possible. This possibility produces knowledge with practical interest. But the problem with such a notion of self-understanding lies in all other cognitive processes that require critical evaluation, such as entities possessing theoretical certainty. Does it theoretically mean that certain cognitive processes can be separated from self-understanding and, thereby, separate knowledge from determination of interest? This drive for separating knowledge from 'interests' produced through self-reflection is an integral part of 'self-formation' that cannot be ushered in with the processes of self-reflection. So, the question arises, What kind of 'interest' is that which aims at freeing knowledge from all human interests? Habermas' answer sets up the project of emancipation.

Only in an emancipated society, whose members' autonomy and responsibility has been realised, would communication develop into the non-authoritarian and universally practised dialogue from which both our model of reciprocally constituted ego-identity and an idea of true consensus are implicitly derived:

> (...) The ontological illusion of pure theory behind which knowledge-constitutive interest becomes invisible promotes the fiction that Socratic dialogue is possible everywhere and at any time.[20]

The Validity of Lived Experience

What Habermas drives home is that emancipatory interest stems out of a critical self-reflection that organises self-interest as constitutive of that reflection and hence can dissociate itself from such interest. The technical and practical interests promote a kind of self-understanding that hinges upon calculated interests. Once again, Habermas seems to give greater importance to an impartial and value-neutral mechanism of cognition, which is constituted intersubjectively with just a contingent reflection on self-interest. This mode of reflection guarantees the connection between theoretical knowledge and the object domain of practical life, which bears the marks of systematically distorted communication as thinly legitimised repression.[21] What Habermas does here once again is a subjection of life-world self-reflection, that is reflection on lived experience under emancipating cognitive abilities, thereby meaning interest-free interests, which signify an interest-free domain of knowledge that would prevail now in the life-world. Here again, intersubjective self-understanding of the life-world is given a rationalised expression that gives itself to the logic of the system by giving up its own cultural mores. This giving up of cultural mores acquires a theoretical giving up of culture bound norms at the altar of rationalisation mostly guided by the logic of system. But Habermas does it with a subtler theoretical ploy when he affirms:

> It is, therefore, more plausible to assume that the objectivity of experience guarantees not the truth of a corresponding statement, but the identity of experience in the various statements, interpreting that experience.[22]

This notion of interpreting experience acts in both ways: on the one hand, it gives an interpretation following the rationalisation of the system, and on the other, it interprets the rationalisation of the system in terms of life-world values and norms. It shows how experience is caught between life world and system and gets anchored in the truth of a statement about it. Down further, such statements become theoretical by the adequacy of language as a function of truth of these statements. Therefore, the interpretation arises as a function of truth of these statements of experience. Further becoming a function of truth, which is of three kinds, being related to differentiated spheres of the life-world makes interpretation a matter of validity.[23] This transformation of interpretation into validity claims detaches the component of lived experience to disinterested cognitive claims. This detachment of lived experience in interest-free cognitive claims is also accorded the shape of a set of rules followed in expressing the lived experiences in statements that link up similar experience in analogous statements. This further makes possible common judgements about statements of experience with well-defined meanings. Such meanings express an intersubjective state of understanding forged by similar claims about similar experiences. This is a reconstruction of the object domain through critical self-reflection, which implies a discursive redeeming of validity claims from an intersubjectively constituted life-world. This occurs at two levels: at one level, denotative expressions of language must be able to identify things and happenings, and at another level, such denotative expressions must be able to identify persons and their utterances. These two levels are differentiated in critical self-reflection as a rendering of sensory experience and communicative experience, respectively. Habermas suggests an implicit connection of both these levels that could be related to various systemic operations through which they could be manipulated, while communicative experiences relate to linguistically-manifest conceptual analysis and immanent critique to point out that the role of linking action-related experiences to the realm of theoretical and practical discourse could be turned into knowledge constitutive interest. Such giving of 'roles' to knowledge constitutive interests serves the purpose of a rational analytical reconstruction of the domain of objects, actions and communication from any 'given' and 'constituted' realm. Unlike an analysis of rule of action or communication, such reconstructive analysis brings out the presuppositions behind constitution of a domain and interest involved in it in order to reconstruct it in terms of practical and theoretical concerns. Such a reconstruction is derivative to those practical and theoretical frameworks that produce actions of a certain kind, yet it serves the larger interest of an integration of life-world and system in terms of universalisable forms of knowledge and truth. Arriving at such universalisable and yet contextually groundable claims of knowledge and truth is emancipatory in the Habermasian sense.

Communication, Norm and Discourse: An Ethical Consensus

What Habermas gives a sense to is the linguistically mediated form of action[24] that appears and functions in terms of a set of rules, in Wittgensteinian terms, what becomes a rule-following activity. Explanation in terms of rule-following activity makes knowledge constitutive interests 'communicative' as it can take the form of a counterfactual reconstruction by incorporating a symmetric and systematic way of using rationale, which would ensure universalisable claims of truth and knowledge. Such universalisable claims, for Habermas, ensures infallibility of knowledge. In social theory, reconstruction of such counterfactual conditions serves as a tool for critiquing partiality of the normative explanation of social facts/events as well as a critique of an exclusivist conception of knowledge that demands rule-following in understanding the conditions of the possibility of knowing. Habermas precisely gives rise to the criteria of 'universalisability' and 'communicability' to be satisfied only in a complete deciphering of how the use of language preserves within it certain rules of communication which are 'universalisable' and such rules held within language reproduce life-world norms and integrate them with the various differentiated subsystems of a modern society. Habermas frames such rules to ensure the possibility of interaction of all controversial participants in a practical discourse such that rules governing actual actions of various participants in a social action can be discursively redeemed. What Habermas aims at through this discursive redeeming is an epistemological redeeming of the cognitive competence of every human individual who could possibly participate in a discourse, which stands as an analogy for actual decisions to perform a certain thing, which is integrally related to the whole process of socialisation. Such an epistemological redeeming is simultaneously a critique of these theories that only explains the conditions of knowing and a reconstruction of the extralinguistic situation of action and society that combines three modes of cognition: objective, subjective and intersubjective. Such an epistemic redeeming entails resolving the is/ought, fact/value dichotomy that insinuates the sphere of knowledge and action and it seeks to give rise to the inseparability of truth and virtue, facts and values, theory and practice. Such an inseparability through an anticipated linguistic mediation of social interaction gives rise to (1) an intersubjectively shared world and (2) an individuated social world. Habermas terms these consequences of anticipated linguistic mediation as 'moral intuitions' of taking an 'ideal role'. Such an ideal role comes through using language in such a way that it is also intelligible to someone, that is not merely stating how things stand, but stating it in such a way 'that in a speech situation, the speaker and bearer understand what is being said in the statement'.[25] This is possible only when the three things are performed by making a statement: (1) the speaker refers to something in the objective world, (2) refers to something in the social world, and (3) the speaker refers to something of his own. If a statement does not perform these three things, for example, what is performed is just the establishment of a relationship between language and the world, then it becomes a cognitive relationship without a proper performance of the role of language. What Habermas assumes is that language works by establishing not only a relationship with the world, but also by establishing a connection with someone else who understands its use. Understanding by someone else occurs only when one listener (someone else) understands the complex relationship between language, speaker, hearer and word in a speech situation.

Habermas theorises such a speech situation in ethical terms by grounding an ethics in the speech situation, called discourse ethics. Every utterance made by a speaker assumes a normative character presented in the validity claims that are cognitively testable[26] and bears a double structure consisting of a performative and a prepositional content. Such utterances ensure communication of a true state of affairs to be shared by the hearer as a statement of knowledge and to be agreed further that the utterance should give the impression to the hearer that it is uttered with sincerity so that there is no inhibition on the part of the listener to accept it as a mark of the hearer's sincerity. This is how the validity claim involved in an utterance involves the recognition by the hearer in terms of either/or such that the truth claim is either true or false, the normative claim is either right or wrong and the truthfulness claim is either sincere or insincere. So, based on such validity claims, there is a possibility of reading mutual understanding in terms of sharing a common perspective, sense or meaning of the world, the shared life-world and one's own world. Such a speech act can only be offered as a proposal for fostering a desired engagement.

These characteristics of a speech situation are taken by Habermas as an argumentative situation that has an unavoidable normative character. Habermas situates such normative character in a hypothetically constructed ideal speech situation that gives rise to some rationally requisite conditions. It gives rise to two basic conditions. One, symmetry, which stipulates that each participant bears a symmetric relationship with the other, that is each has an equal access to initiate and continue the argument. The second is reciporocity, which is concerned with the rights and duties of fresh participants, that is each one has equal right in the discourse situation and can conduct themselves in such a manner that untruthfulness, duplicity and subordination do not occur. Restricting the discourse situation only to better arguments alone imposes these conditions. Further, these conditions give rise to the stipulation of validity to 'norms' by which discourse is to be conducted:

> Only those norms can claim to be valid that meet (or could meet) with the approval of all affected in their capacity as participants in a practical discourse. This stipulation of validity calls for an elaborate justification procedure, which Habermas articulated in terms of counterfactual conditions:[27]

(3.1) Every subject with the competence to speak and act is allowed to take part in a discourse.
(3.2) a. Everyone is allowed to question as assertion whatever;
b. Everyone is allowed to introduce any assertion whatever into the discourse, and
c. Everyone is allowed to express his attitudes, desires and needs.
(3.3) No speaker may be prevented by internal or external coercion from exercising his rights laid down in (3.1) and (3.2).[28]

Such counterfactual conditions and the requirement for idealised speech are linguistic competence (3.1), symmetrical distribution of rights to argue (3.2) and reciprocal recognition of each other's rights by members of a communication community (3.3). From these counterfactual conditions, Habermas claims to 'deduce' the universalisability principal of argumentation (U):

> For a norm to be valid, the consequence and side-effects that its general observance can be said to have for the satisfaction of the particular interests of each person affected must be such that all affected can accept them freely.[29]

Everyone in a discourse situation calls the principle 'U' a consensus principle as the second stipulates that acting according to 'U' guarantees the conditions of possibility for free consent. Such a procedural and formal stipulation of conditions and principle of universalisability in a transcendental-pragmatic analysis of the necessary conditions and principles involved in argumentation provides final justification for making an argumentative claim. But such a justification procedure involves a logical trilemma; (1) the principle of justification must itself again be justified, (2) the principle that is to be justified is already presupposed in its justification, and (3) dogmatisation of a principle that is not to be unjustified any more. This trilemma hints at the inherent problems of Habermas' formal procedural deduction of 'U'. But Habermas advances the safeguards of a contextualised normative basis in any rational argumentation. He says:

> It would be utterly pointless to engage in a practical discourse without a horizon provided by the life-world of a specific social group and without real conflicts in a concrete situation in which the actors consider it incumbent upon them to reach a consensual means of regulating some controversial social matter.[30]

Churning Out an Ethics of Discourse

Such a contextualised 'necessity' is further formalised in Habermas' derivation of the necessity of practical discourse as 'D', the principle of discourse ethics:

> Only those norms can claim to be valid that meet (or can meet) with the approval of all concerned in their capacity as participants in a practical discourse.[31]

This principle of discourse ethics 'D' presupposes 'U' and acts as the formal-procedural justification of the choice of norms of argumentation. This normative basis ensures that there is no necessity for providing a moral justification for following norms if the presuppositions of rational argumentation are followed. So, Habermas' answer to a moral sceptic who does not appreciate such presuppositions is to show that the sceptic would invite a "performative contradiction" if such norms were not followed. For a sceptic who asserts "I do not exist" gets involved into a *petitio principi* by asserting the opposite of what s/he must tacitly assume in order to make the assertion in the first place. Habermas extends this notion of 'performative contradiction' in justifying the validity of presuppositions like symmetry and reciprocity underlying all argumentation. Habermas suggests that a moral sceptic would asserts something like this:

> Having excluded persons A, B, C ... from the discussion by silencing them or by foisting an interpretation on them, we were able to convince ourselves that N (a norm) is justified.[32]

Habermas' reply to the sceptic is that this exclusion of some persons involves a performative contradiction, as it churns out two contradictory premises: (1) Not everyone has a right to participate (namely A, B, C ......) and (2) Everyone including the sceptic has a right to participate. Further, Habermas proves that the conditions of symmetry and reciprocity are moral norms of discourse by asserting that without symmetry, there cannot be a formal equality between subjects, and without reciprocity, nobody would recognise the other, and without such a recognition, one's own moral claims, virtues and acts would turn otiose. Further symmetry ensures an egalitarian friendship by establishing the behavioural expectations of participants, without which, such expectations would become non-symmetrical behavioural expectations of a different kind.[33] Therefore, Habermas consolidates moral norms of symmetry and reciprocity as the conditions of justice.

Symmetry gives rise to 'solidarity' and 'reciprocity' ensures a common participation in the needs felt by members of a society, as it opens up the interpretation given to a specific need by a person to interpretations by others.[34] This is the way in which symmetry and reciprocity conditions are linked with each other. Similarly, solidarity and justice are linked in a transcendental-pragmatic way:

> To be sure, fundamental notions of equal treatment, solidarity and general welfare, which are central to all moralities, are built into the conditions of symmetry and expectations of reciprocity of every ordinary communicative practice.[35]

Therefore, Habermas gives justification of normative assumptions of discourse ethics by involving the counterfactual conditions of an 'ideal speech situation', which acts as an indispensable normative foundation for any successful communicative action, which is undistorted by systemic interventions. The justification does not require any further justification as it jibes with facets of behaviour, expectations and community. Further, Habermas considers that following the universalisability principle, 'U', the participant of a discourse can arrive at a rational consensus in which every participant can take part in the process of reasoning in which only better arguments will prevail. Such a rationally arrived at consensus foreseeable in the process of argumentation can keep the discourse going, and this will ultimately bring in a consensus acceptable to all because of its great force of reason. This is how the anticipated communication that we may have with others finally come to a rational agreement or 'consensus'. But this poses a problem of presupposing a morality of consensus within the normative contents of principle of argumentation, which discourse ethics is supposed to ground in its 'U' principle. If one does not impute a certain normative content to the principles of argumentation, then such content is smuggled into the theory of communicative action by creating a strict universal principle of symmetry and reciprocity. The problem can be overcome without destroying the core normative content of discourse ethics by jettisoning 'U', as proposed by Seyla Benhabib:

> 'D' (the central premise of discourse ethics), together with those rules of argument governing discourses, the normative content of which I summarised as the principles of universal moral respect and egalitarian reciprocity, are in my view quite adequate to serve as the only universalisability test.[36]

The counterfactual conditions, together with the better argument rule followed in discourses, form the central premise of the following norms of argumentation as it puts 'U' before rules of argumentation and the normative conditions associated with it. Therefore, one retains 'U' only as an interactive universalisable principle without its telos of consensus. But by accepting 'U' as an interactive principle of universalisability, one can arrive at complementarity between symmetry as formal equality and reciprocity as recognition built into the processes of interaction. But accepting 'U' as a substantive universalisable principle of validity claims made through argumentative speech-acts would only serve the purpose of deriving 'U' as a trans-contextual transcendental principle that ensures procedural consensus. Such a procedural consensus only promotes the communicative purpose of 'convincing' the other person in the course of discussion. Michael Wreen's extremely humorous example[37] of such convincing in the case of a child believing that (1) there is a Santa Claus and (2) Santa Claus brings gifts only to those who have faith in him showed how rational-epistemic grounds of acceptance of an argument of this kind leads to a conviction that stands on sound epistemic grounds. Yet such grounds involve a performative contradiction of a priori knowledge of truth of a certain argumentative premise. Therefore, the knowledge of neither norms nor facts precedes in a substantive universal sense to justify norms of argumentation and the consensus flowing from it. One way to get rid of this lack of a priori knowledge of truth is to talk about only 'interactive universals' like the case of Santa Claus, which becomes convincing to everybody in the given mode of argumentation. Another way is to presuppose knowledge of truth, but that will exclude others who do not know 'truth' from the domain of interaction. Therefore, it is the rights that participants can claim and the duties that make them accountable are substantive matters, instead of turning it to a principle of building consensus through rational argumentation.

Habermas, therefore, amends this principle of discourse ethics, 'D', in terms of its legitimacy, which lies at a different level from moral/ethical presuppositions of rational argumentation. As a principle of impartial justification, it underlines both morality and laws to make itself legitimate. The idea of legitimacy gives the notion of validity a different interpretation by privileging 'right' over 'good'. This makes discourse ethics integrationist as well as critical, as it combines deliberative ethical discourses that reflect the substantive values of a community in order to determine what is good with those acceptable norms that safeguard the interests of the community formalised as laws. Further, it quells the danger of reducing these two modes of practical discourse into one another and ensures a distinction between moral and evaluative questions.[38] The moral questions perform the role of interpretation and the legal questions perform the role of determining rightness, and both combined together make practical decisions possible. This amendment of 'U' through 'D' and a further amendment of 'D' in terms of morality and legality bridge the gap between the normative and the legitimate, and at the same time retain their autonomy by maintaining the scope of argumentation from each of these perspectives.

The Priority of the Legitimate: Dispelling a Crisis

One can read here the priority of socially legitimate norms over judgement of value and knowledge, an upturning of the precedence of theory over practice.[39] This upturns the method of identity-thinking that self-referentially incorporates within itself the totality it is trying to grasp and demands justification of all premises within itself.[40] In other words, the theoretical description of individuals as part of a social whole impels autonomous decisions of individuals as derivative from collective decision. This also has the bearing of upturning the priority of practical reason on social practice. Rather a concept of reason transposed into a linguistic medium presents a different potential for reconstruction when interactions are woven together in the linguistic medium to structure the 'form of life'. Such a transposition of reason into a linguistic medium removes its metaphysical burdens like describing knowledge of reality in a substantial sense and establishes a justificatory basis in terms of subjective or objective grounds. It produces a procedural justification and ground for holding knowledge or idea of reality in terms of its relationship with various aspects of the world. Such a procedural justification makes possible rediscovery of reason in a world that is itself rationally structured. Such rationality turns purely formal as it can take care of the rationally structured world in the validity of results. Such results ensure solution of problems through procedurally suitably dealings with reality. What such suitable dealing mean is that each sphere of life achieves autonomy and is assigned a particular domain which Habermas described in a tripartite division (truth, rightness and beauty) of the world and identified with a kind of rationality: cognitive instrumental precedence, moral-practical and aesthetic-expressive. Habermas' attribution of precedence to normative rightness over good shows a different order of rationality, a rationality that looks for socially legitimate and interactive universals of reason. Such a mode of universalisation obviously prioritises social practice, which is normative in so far as 'communicatively acting individuals must commit themselves to pragmatic presuppositions of a counterfactual sort'.[41] Explicating it further, Habermas stressed:

> They must undertake certain idealisation – for example, ascribe identical meaning to expressions, connect utterances with context-transcending validity claims, and assure that addresses are accountable, that is autonomous and sincere with both themselves and others (......)unavoidable idealisations form the counterfactual basis of an actual practice of reaching understanding, a practice that can critically turn against its own results and thus transcends itself.[42]

Such idealisation of norms stretches across the entire spectrum of validity claims to reach beyond moral practical questions and it is in this 'going beyond' that normativity achieves an obligatory orientation of action.[43] Therefore, normativity does not coincide with communicative rationality, which justifies reaching an understanding through action. Reaching an understanding in sociological terms operates between the alternatives of forcibly stabilised versus rationally legitimised understanding in a pre-differentiated society. Following a procedure that brings about a legitimate conception of reality for a modern and differentiated society will give rise to a suitable context for discourse ethics. Habermas theorises such a context in terms of a postmetaphysical framework of reason. Such a framework assigns a role for reason only in its expressive dimension, the dimension in which it expresses some context in language and such an expression is embodied in social facts. Such contexts assume a form of representation that is prepositionally structured. Such contexts are not mere individual mental states, but they are governed by rules in such a manner that some type or form emerges from these contexts. This identicality of propositions ensures that representations in linguistic form are determinate. This marks an important shift from having a correct picture of reality in one's consciousness to its representation in stable structures of language. It replaces the two-world structure of philosophy or consciousness with a subjectless working of language to represent the reality. Such a subjectless working of language develops into an intersubjectively recognisable and identical structure of representation that acquires its validity through its recognisability by everyone alike. Such recognisability hints at the ideal moment of concept formation that gives rise to identicality of meaning and interpretation. It further indicates at a process of reasoning that develops a shared understanding within a social community. What Habermas locates here is an internal transcendence by which users of language transcend the particularities of a context and arrive at a general fit. For example, the representation of a fact in language like 'This ball is red' brings out a meaning/significance that stands for representing the same thing in all possible contexts. This brings in an unconditional meaning of truth-claims once it is represented in language. Such an unconditional meaning of truth-claims in the diversity of linguistic realisation is an idealisation built into truth-claims, which, according to Habermas:

> confronts us with the more ambitious tasks of explaining, in terms of the pragmatic conditions of argumentation, how the validity claim raised (...) and aimed at intersubjective recognition or acceptance can, at the same time,, overshoot local standards for taking yes/no positions, that is standards that have become established in each particular community of interpreters.[43]

This is what Habermas calls the 'transcendental moment of unconditionality', which gives rise to an argumentative practice of justification to be distinguished from other practices regulated by social conventions. Such a practice of argumentation is an embodiment of the universal in a discourse of an unbound community of interpretation. This kind of universal discourse move into the presuppositions of communications, which all interpreters, actors and participants of an intersubjective field of communication should accept de facto. Such an acceptance is marked by the explication of idealisations connected with expression. Such idealisations are accessible to a pragmatic analysis of the use of language oriented to reaching understanding as a mechanism of action coordination through counterfactual presuppositions of actors who orient their action to validity claims that exist through the preservation of social order. This detranscendentalises counterfactual presuppositions only to have an 'idealising force' of context-transcending anticipation at one level, which relies on the acceptance of certain norms by participants of a discourse. At another level, such an anticipation determines the contribution of social reality in such a way that:

> every communicatively achieved agreement - which makes possible the coordination of actions, the complex build-up of interactions, and the weaving together of action sequences—takes as its yardstick the intersubjective recognition of criticisable validity claims.[44]

Such validity claims transcend social validity in its situation in the processes of communication that make them universalisable. But as no contextual validity claims are possible, they have to be grounded only in the binding act of acceptance of such a claim within a social context or community, which gives them detranscendentalising legitimacy. This legitimacy has to serve the condition of validity in such a way that it embodies within it the claims of truth of any particular communicative utterance.

In the world of social fact, there is a continual tension between validity as facticity and validity as legitimacy with a communicative situation. This tension is bridged by the integrating capacity of communicative action, which meets two contradictory conditions: On the one hand, strategically ace behaviour should be brought to what is objectively desirable, and on the other, it must develop socially integrating force by establishing intersubjectively recognised normative validity claims. These two conditions are jointly satisfied by validity as truth and validity as legitimacy. In other words, these conditions are jointly satisfied by normativity and legality, which would be overdetermined by objectively valid truths. But with reason, the facticity-validity tension inhabiting language and its use penetrate society. Such a penetration is amply there in the communicative action circumscribed by those intuitive background certainties that are accepted without question because they are uncoupled from any communicatively accessible reasons. Such behaviour stabilising and intuitively acceptable assumptions of communication put restrictions upon communicative actions that in principle subject all norms and values to critical testing.

Discourse Ethics: Does it Require a Utopian Justification?

These communicatively obtainable justified norms have much less in common with an integrationist communitarian ethic that turns to the monolithic value-system of traditions and has a greater affinity with a participationist communitarian ethic that encourages collective deliberation about generalisable interests, which at the same time preserves the autonomous agency characteristic of modernism.[45] Such presentation of autonomous agency bases itself upon setting normative standards through collective deliberation, which Habermas articulates as 'all forces except the force of the better argument and all motives except the cooperative search for the right solution.'[46] This gives a further pointer to Habermas' conflation between linguistically mediated and intersubjectively valid moral norms. This happens because of Habermas' assumption that power, deceit and self-interest are external to communicative action and hence communicative action is related to solidarity of the community. Through such a distinction, Habermas preserves a participatory sense of community.

Habermas makes a powerful critique of the possibility of performing strategic actions through perlocutionary speech-acts in Austin by way of pointing out that illocutionary speech acts carry their effect along with their speaking out, while the effect of perlocutionary speech is produced via illocution.

Habermas points out that the perlocutionary speech-acts lose their intersubjective character as relations of mutual recognition are secondary to it, while such relations are a prioritisation of illocutionary over perlocutionary that establish the privilege of normative validity upon objective validity and constrain perlocutionary through intersubjective legitimacy.[46]

Habermas gives credit to the Wittgensteinian dictum that 'the meaning of a word is its use in language', which invokes a rule-following use of words, which comprises linguistic expression and non-linguistic activities that are interwoven with it. Therefore rule-following gives rise to not just an externalism of behaviour, but a self-referential intentional explanation of linguistic mediation, and such intentionality requires a mutual warrant of understanding, which Habermas formulated thus:

> A linguistic expression can only have an identical meaning for a subject who is capable together with at least one additional subject, of following a rule that is valid for both of them.[47]

Such a rule-following validity gives rise to a concept of language that attributes no essential meaning to the fact that what is expressed in language always transcends the boundary of language and relates to something in the world. But it gives significance to a truth-claim 'p' made by a speaker to the hearer by the 'binding character of obligatory declarations of intention'.[48] Such an intentionality in-built in illocutionary speech-acts gives rise to a referential relationship between what it says and the world and also constitutes a relationship of intentionality between the speaker and the hearer. But such an intentional and referential relationship, for Habermas, gives rise to the possibility for justification of any accepted moral norms in a self-referential manner.

The programme for justification compels a derivation of rational norms from intentional speech-acts by both presuppositions of its validity as well as from the possibility of reaching an understanding. Within these two folds of the programme of justification, there is 'a more detailed specification of what we intuitively appeal to when we justify a moral action or an underlying norm'. This combines morality with rationality. Such an internal connection between morality with its rationally justifiable grounds contained in speech-acts constitutes the rational foundation of normative validity.[50] This also explains why discourse overlays communication oriented to reaching understanding as its reflective form in the symmetry conditions and reciprocity expectations of everyday speech oriented to reach understanding.[51]

Such orientation to reach understanding provides the overwhelming ethical grounds for presupposing the norms of conducting a discourse that serves a unifying role to bring together various actors of society in a communicative situation. This juxtaposes plural life-worlds and forms of life with their irreducible plurality in an unconditional context-transcending normative manner, the manner in which subjectivity and internationality are not prior to, but a function of forms of, life and systems of language. They do not 'constitute' the world, but are themselves elements of a linguistically disclosed world.[52]

Refiguring Modernity

Such a disclosure of the world in its linguistic constitution gives rise to several possibilities for Habermas. On the one hand, the structurally differentiated modern social system with which the life-world gets differentiated as various subsystems, and on the other, the integrated world such a differentiated social system re-creates through mediations of language. Such linguistic mediation reproduces the logic of social systems only to be mediated by the norms of the life-world, and hence, negotiates the two ends in the horizon of a historically mediated meaning. Such historically mediated meaning revolves against the conventionally normative structuration of the life-world and exposes it to the imperatives of the system. This is not just a normative or moral activity, but an activity that rejects the archaic in order to refresh it in a newer form and this places the burden of dissolution of a past tradition on an expression of rebellion. Modernity carries out this rebellion in two ways: on the one hand, it rebels against the past, and on the other, it fosters a new form to enforce a different medium of expression. Habermas calls it a longing for stripping away all that is conventional and a striving to become an impersonal scrivener:

> Two things are expressed: the genuine experience of the process of world-disclosing, or the linguistic innovation that allows us to see with other eyes what happens in the world; but also the desire to overdraw this aesthetic experience, to totalise the contact with the extraordinary, to absorb the everyday.[53]

This contact with the extraordinary is an aesthetic mode in which other spheres of life such as normative and scientific hunt for 'ever newer horizons of experience and of different ways'.[54] Such newer horizons are manifested in the form of productivity of world-disclosing linguistic medium in artworks and totalises them in a concept of language. This concept of language always problematises the existing normative standards and opens up two possibilities: one, to give up the project of modernity, and two, to hold modernity immune to justification and validation. Both these possibilities, Habermas argues:

> (...) Observe the decline of substantive reason, the differentiation of science, morality and art, the modern world-view and its mere procedural rationality, with sadness and recommend a withdrawal to a position anterior to modernity.[54]

Such a position, Habermas calls 'anti-modernity', which has a tendency to go back to premodern and metaphysical culture as an alternative to existing cultures. Such alternatives establish a different kind of relationship, the relationship between fiction and reality, a reality that is intended in the narrative. Habermas characterises this relationship in terms of disappearance of a stable sense of reality through a transcendental subjectivity and such a disappearance produces a blurring of genre distinctions between levels of reality, between fiction and reality, between everyday practice and extraordinary experience. Such a blurring produces a problem of amalgamation of disparate experiences in the life-world and the system and such an amalgamation produces a confrontation between the differentiated spheres of life, which is unleashed in an undirected linguistic current characteristic of modernity.

But Habermas worries about the discrepancy between linguistic mediation and repudiation of subjectivity, which portrays a concealed normative sentiment, expressed by him as:

> Whether modernity is described as a constellation of life that is reified and used, or as one that is technologically manipulated, or as one that is totalitarian, rife with power, homogenised, imprisoned – the denunciation is constantly inspired by a special sensitivity for complex injuries ad subtle violation.[55]

Such a special sensitivity constitutes the modern concept of reason and validity to make us 'conscious of the formations of the life-world'[56]. The non-objective background of the life-world that evades the grasp of theoretical objectification co-exists with the 'explosive experiences of the extraordinary'[57] and this co-existence, for Habermas, for the time being, eludes 'the explanatory forces of philosophical language and continues to resist translation into reasoning discourses'.[58]

Notes

1. Jurgen Habermas, *Postmetaphysical Thinking*, trans. W.M. Hohengarten, Cambridge, Massachusetts, 1992, p. 36. Henceforth, *PMT*. Here Habermas looks for those aspects of meaning that are neither objective, nor hermeneutic, but something in which it can circulate without constraint.
2. Jurgen Habermas, *Justification and Application*, trans. Ciaran Cronin, Polity Press, Cambridge, 1993, p. 74. Henceforth, *JA*.
3. Jurgen Habermas, "Philosophy as Stand-In and Interpreter" in *Moral Consciousness and Communicative Action*, trans. C. Lenahardt and S.W.

Nicholsen, MIT Press, Cambridge, Massachusette, 1990, pp. 1-20, see p. 77. Henceforth *MCCA*.

4. Jurgen Habermas, *The Theory of Communicative Action,* Vol. II, trans. T. McCarthy, Polity Press, Cambridge, 1987, p. 117. Henceforth, *TCA*.
5. *MCCA*, p. 136.
6. *TCA*, Vol. II, pp. 124-5.
7. *TCA*, Vol. I, p. 340.
8. *TCA*, Vol. II, p. 242.
9. *TCA*, Vol. II, p. 192.
10. *TCA*, Vol. I, p. 341.
11. *TCA*, Vol. II, p. 120.
12. *TCA*, Vol. II, p. 122.
13. *TCA*, Vol. II, p. 274.
14. *TCA*, Vol. II, p. 281.
15. *TCA*, Vol. II, p. 122.
16. *TCA*, Vol. II, p. 281.
17. *TCA*, Vol. II, p. 333.
18. Jurgen Habermas, *Knowledge and Human Interests,* trans. Jeremy J. Shapiro, Beacon Press, Boston, 1971, p. 308. Henceforth. *KHI.*
19. "Postscript" to *KHI*, trans. C. Lendhardt, *Philosophy of the Social Sciences*, Vol. 3 (1979), p. 176. Henceforth, *PS.*
20. *PS,* p. 176.
21. *KHI,* p. 197.
22. *PS,* p. 174.
23. Jurgen Habermas, "Toward a Theory of Communicative Competence", in *Recent Sociology,* No. 2, ed. H. P. Dreitzel, Macmillan, New York, 1970, p. 146.
24. *MCCA*, p. 199.
25. *MCCA*, p. 24.
26. Jurgen Habermas, "A reply to My Critics" in *Habermas: Critical Debates,* B. Thompson and D. Held (eds.), Macmillan, London, 1982, pp. 219-283, see pp. 270-1. Henceforth, *Reply.*
27. *MCCS,* p. 91.
28. Jurgen Habermas, "Discourse Ethics: Notes on a Program of Philosophical Justification" in *MCCA,* pp. 87-89.Henceforth, *DE.*
29. *MCCS,* p. 120.
30. *DE,* p. 100.
31. *DE,* p. 90.
32. *DE,* p. 91.

33. *MCCS*, p. 147.
34. Jurgen Habermas, "Justice and Solidarity: On the Concerning Stage-6" in *The Philosophical Forum*, XXI: 1-2: 32-51, p. 49. Henceforth, *JS*.
35. *JS*, p. 47.
36. Seyla Benhabib, *Situating the Self*, Routledge, New York, 1992, p. 37.
37. Michael Wreen, "Yes, Virginia, There is a Santa Claus", *Informal Logic*, 9, 1987, pp. 34-39.
38. *DE*, p. 105.
39. *PMT*, p. 32.
40. *PMT*, p. 33.
41. Jurgen Habermas, *Between Facts and Norms: Contributions to a Discourse Theory of Law and Democracy*, trans. W. Rehg, Polity Press, Cambridge, 1995, p.4. Henceforth, *FN*.
42. *FN*, p. 4.
43. *FN*. P, 15.
44. *FN*, p. 20.
45. Seyla Benhabib, "Autonomy, Modernity and Community: Communitarianism and Critical Theory in Dialogue" in *Zwischenbetrachtungen im Prozess der Aufklarung*, ed. Axel Honneth et al., Sukhramo; Frankfurt, 1988, pp. 373-391.
46. T. McCarthy, *The Critical Theory of Jurgen Habermas*, MIT Press, Cambridge, Massachusetts, 1981, p. 321.
47. *PMT*, p. 68.
48. *PMT*, p. 71.
49. *PMT*, p. 73.
50. *JA*, p. 32.
51. *JA*, p. 41.
52. T. McCarthy, "Introduction" in Jurgen Habermas, *Philosophical Discourse of Modernity*, Polity Press, Cambridge, 1987, p. ix. Henceforth *PDM*.
53. *PMT*, p. 216.
54. Jurgen Habermas, "Modernity - An Incomplete Project", trans. S. Benhabib in, *Postmodern Culture*, ed. Hal Foster, Pluto Press, London, 1985, pp. 3.15. see pp. 14-15.
55. *PDM*, p. 337.
56. *PMT*, p. 50.
57. *PMT*, p. 51.
58. *PMT*, p. 51.

V

Critical Polemics – I: Habermas' Critique of Rorty and Derrida

*Response, Counter-critique and Counter-response****

The purpose of this chapter is to bring out a critique of postmodern suspension of knowledge, communication and meaning through Habermas' re-assertion of the normative framework of communicative rationality. The main questions that I ask here are whether the postmodern claim of holistic function of knowledge takes care of the possibility of meaningful communication and whether the modern concept of formal-procedural rationality explains the possibility of fuzzy forms of communication, that is communication through unstable contexts of meaning? Though the two questions try to situate an answer in the other camp, they do not close the possibility of a fresh look into their own perspective in meeting the uncomfortable situation pointed out by the logic of the other camp. Therefore, the questions are not merely directed towards the Achilles' heel of the opposing camp, but they address the objections raised by the other camp. To draw a picture of what went on between Habermas, Rorty and Derrida, this chapter focusses on Habermas' critique of the other camp by taking his critiques of Rorty and Derrida separately and then charting out the responses of Rorty and Derrida. Next, the chapter focusses upon Rorty's and Derrida's critique of Habermas, taking each at a time, and charting out Habermas' response to them. Finally, the chapter leaves open the scope of conclusively drawing a common thematic from this sequence of critique, response, counter-critique and counter-response. The chapter tentatively concludes without reducing the battle lines to compromises and points to the open field of interpretation. For the purpose of the thesis, I draw the broad implications from the battle lines drawn between modern and postmodern critique of knowledge by way of citing irresolvable issues than by offering straightjacketed solutions.

Habermas' 'Crisis' Point of View

Habermas' basic presupposition that the development of language is isomorphic to the development of community produces the idea that the normative structure of the community finds its place in the very structure of language. Habermas' social theory aims at establishing this isomorphism by negotiating the divergence of developments in community and language, the former gets differentiated into distinct spheres of the cognitive, moral and aesthetic, while the latter assumes three different roles in correspondence with such a differentiation. But there are 'systemic' forces that integrate three different spheres necessitating that language play a unifying role through its various uses. Such a role of language brings forth an immanent critique of differentiation of spheres of society in terms of knowledge and action and goes for a re-construction of the life-world meanings, the basic stratum of the normative structure of society. Therefore, Habermas posits a crisis of differentiation to be met by re-construction of meanings in language and his project consists of these two reciprocal and interlinked poles. Interestingly, Habermas considers that the possibility of overcoming the differentiation of spheres through re-construction in language resuscitates an agenda of emancipation in the heart of the modern social system. For Habermas, this agenda is worth pursuing both philosophically and politically.

Habermas assigns the role of mediation to philosophy in one of the poles where differentiation of spheres produces the threat of disintegration of society at large, which could be possibly performed by it if it can ensure that the conditions of differentiation are properly negotiated through some universal norms that found the society. Such a mediative role involves a critique of the rationality of differentiation compounded with a re-affirmation of those fundamental norms that can reintegrate the differentiated sphere. Both these aspects are rivetted together in Habermas' singular project of an unending project of modernity taking two different turns: one, in the form of an immanent/inside critique of differentiation/fragmentation, and the other, in the form of reformulating these fundamental and common norms that are responsible for the sharing of a common medium of communication that unites all the diverse factors and interests in the very act of communication. These two directions of critique are aimed at uniting the cognitive, moral and aesthetic dimensions of modern social life, which could only be known through its objectified nature[1] and not through its essence as available in metaphysics, knowledge of such an objectified nature of the life-world acts as the basis of reproduction of the structures of the life-world in communication. This is how Habermas grants a transcendental status to communication and develops a leap of faith in the potential of communicative action to arrive at mutual understanding between every member of society through the recognition of criticisable validity claims by equally participating in communication.[2]

The question that arises is on Habermas' leap of faith in ascribing communication the role of simultaneously binding up differentiated spheres of society and reproducing the structures of the life-world, which implies a transcendental role for language. By adopting such a point of view, Habermas advances a critique of all those philosophers who do not envisage this kind of convergence between the differentiation of society leading to a single point of view. Habermas makes a critique of Rorty's notion of incommensurable discourses engendered by different criteria of rationality and his laying priority on belief as opposed to knowledge to which 'purposive action and linguistic communication play a qualitatively different role'. This critique of Habermas aims at counterposing the anti-foundational postmodern stance of radical incommensurability between discourses and its abandonment of knowledge in favour of a freewheeling network of belief. Therefore, two perspectives come at each other at daggers drawn, one, carrying the possibility of discourses, and the other, the human subject in the freewheeling of language. But this postmodern project gets divided into various strands like (1) denial of 'historical progress of the human subject', (2) confining the human subject within a tradition, say, within liberalism and (3) engaging the human subject within a process of endless self-overcoming. Habermas makes a critique of all such strands because they surface over a crisis of meaning of self-understanding and communication and neutralises them in a project of normative re-integration of differentiated spheres.

Critique of Rorty and Rorty's Possible Defences

Habermas makes a critique of Rorty's pragmatic project of assuming 'unlimited freedom to convert the unproblematic background knowledge of our own culture' into objectified action and use of language.[3] This leads to standards by which philosophy is criticised. These standards are taken from the self-sufficient routinised form of life in which philosophy happens to survive for now and gives a credo to Rorty for implanting such a standard. Habermas points at the possible consequences of choosing between a narrowly objectivated science base upon reliable consensus and the other areas of human sciences that interpret the world only through a holistic rational assumption of linkages between differentiated aspects of life. Such a possibility of choice, for Habermas, marks a farewell to philosophy as it merely makes a double entry of 'consensus' and 'inquiry' without a goal that can unify them. Rorty's celebration of an abyss between the two sides in terms of 'interesting and fruitful disagreement' emanating from incommensurable discourses and his characterisation of such a situation as edifying is debunked by Habermas. In his language:

> Such philosophical edification enjoys the benefits of all three types of farewell: therapeutic relief, heroic overcoming and hermeneutic ranking. It combines the inconspicuously subversive force of leisure with an elitist notion of creative linguistic imagination and with the wisdom of ages.[4]

But the moot epistemic question that Habermas raises is, how can Rorty think of a community without having a consensus building approach through rational argumentation in speech? Habermas has precisely pointed out Rorty's abandonment of criteria of the truth and validity, even though he foresees a community based upon mutual agreement and understanding. But Rorty's quip, "Edifying philosophers do not offer argument", is further debuked by Habermas, when, in exploring the grounds of disagreement, he says:

> Convictions can contradict one another only when those who are concerned with problems define them in a similar way, believe them to be in need of resolution and want to decide issues on the basis of good reasons.[5]

But for Rorty, a mere agreement on what is true, good or right has to be believed as sufficient to hold a point of view, instead of resolution of differences in such views through good reasons. Contrastingly, for Habermas, there is no other way to reach an agreement except by way of making oneself a party to the agreement 'on the basis of good reasons', which will also serve the purpose of resolution of disagreements. Further, for Habermas, to raise a validity claim is to proclaim, 'This is so generally and *not just for me or for us*'[6] and it is to point 'beyond the provincial agreements of the specific local contexts',[7] while for Rorty, 'beliefs are in touch with reality', which shows 'the causal, non-intentional, non-representational link between us and the rest of the universe' and ascribes a pragmatic preference for describing beliefs in their own chosen way rather than the way the world is.[8] Habermas contradicts such a causal and context bound agreement by pointing out that Rorty cannot 'consistently replace the implicitly normative conception of valid argument' with the descriptive concept of 'argument held to be true by us at this time', and in doing so, Rorty commits an 'objective fallacy'. In critiquing such a fallacy, Habermas invokes the notion of a valid argument, presupposing 'a moment of the unconditional' that makes an argument valid. It goes this way: Either one has accepted the argument of someone else and sublated her own or vice versa and accepted the force of an argument as valid without conditions. The moments of validity bring in such a notion of unconditionality, without which an argument cannot acquire the status of validity. This notion goes beyond 'argument in a specific context' or even beyond the basic anthropological trust assumed to exist in a human society. Ironically enough, 'the notion of unconditional-ness' comes close to Rorty's acceptance of an 'evidence transcendent notion of truth pace Davidson', even though he refuses to admit 'inner structure' of 'true' sentences. For Rorty, the 'moment of unconditional-ness' is not a condition that transcends 'human capacities' in recognising a statement to be true or false.[9] Rorty's notion of 'evidence-transcendent' is borne out of two epistemic concerns: (1) not allowing a scheme of truth that makes particular instances 'true', and (2) not allowing any tertia like 'states of affairs' or 'definition' to snoop between text and world. Going by such concerns, Rorty blurs the distinction between subject and object, appearance and reality, scheme and content and this is how Rorty's holistic talk about agreement within a larger community coheres between the beliefs of each other and between beliefs not required to decide on matters of agreement and disagreement because such a decision already incorporates our direct contact with the world that gets our belief true or makes an appeal to that which transcends human capacities. Rorty is arguing here at a metaphilosophical level of assigning belief as generally true which takes care of all agreements, disagreements and validity claims. Putting such a metaphilosophical notion of validity before particular validity claims, Rorty formulates his pragmatic criterion of validity in terms of agreement within a community that does not any longer require a criterion of truth to testify its beliefs. It is interesting to note Rorty's argument in disregarding the charge of 'objectivistic fallacy',

> Our language conceived as a web of inferential relationship between our uses of vocable is not, on the view, something 'merely human' which may hide something which 'transcends' human capacities. Nor can it deceive us into thinking ourselves in correspondence with the contrary, using vocables is a direct contact with reality (...) (as direct as kicking rocks). The fallacy comes in thinking that the relationship between vocables and reality has to be piecemeal (like the relation between individual kicks and individual rocks), a matter of discrete component capacities getting in touch with distinct chunks of reality.[10]

Rorty eliminates the chance of relating vocables with pieces of reality by drawing a map of knowledge that already enables us to recognise each other's beliefs in terms of their efficacy in practice. Justification for undistorted communication lies in such recognition of each other's beliefs locked in a sense of community. Habermas' invocation of a 'moment of unconditional' is appropriated by Rorty in such justification as 'detailed practical advantages' showed by members of a society.[11] Such practical advantages do not require a consensus as their legitimate basis nor an underlying normative structure to acquire gains flowing from them, as is required in the case of undistorted communication. So, the 'movement of unconditionality' in Rorty comes through the holistic coherence of belief at a meta-level. Habermas contends that such a movement 'opens us up to criteria from the other point of view', which is supposedly not available within one's own domain of belief. This, in Rorty's view, would be something concealed in an alternative vocabulary or in an 'incommensurable domain' with respect to the practices of a community. Rorty takes into account the other point of view to the extent that it brings in some practical advantages, but not in terms of some common validity claims. But what Habermas raises as a notion of validity claim takes into account the other point of view and this is possible only if we un-condition ourselves from our own point of view and look beyond the local context. This is what McCarthy terms as 'placing ourself in a moment of unconditionality', which Rorty desires within the narrow domains of local agreement.

McCarthy formulates the difference:

> Rorty's position seems to be: as far as the border of a language and no further. (Rorty would actually say, 'the borders of a language game'). Habermas' and Hilary Putnam's view is that there are no such impossible borders; truth claims can be contested indefinitely from an indefinite diversity of points of view, precisely because they claim unconditioned validity.[12]

Habermas reformulates this notion of 'unconditioned' in term of a touch with the 'extraordinary', which I shall touch upon in my discussion of Habermas' critique of Derrida.

Critique of Derrida and Derrida's Response

Habermas reads Derrida in two distinct ways: one, by identifying Derridean deconstruction as transcendental phenomenology, experience in 'disclosures', and two, by marking a departure from the ordinary and everyday use of language to a self-referential literary form. In both these ways, the butt of Habermas' critique is Derrida's reification of reason to the height of a paradoxical mystique and then equating it with the subliminal powers of literature.

In his first mode of reading, Habermas conceived 'deconstruction' as a move beyond the temporalised philosophy of origin, similar to Heidegger's project of welcoming the origin of being in language, but dissimilar in regard to the internal trace of difference between the 'disclosure' and its 'object'. The being, for Derrida, appears in a sequence of disclosures, each time with a difference of identity and this is what Habermas conceives as a different way of world-projecting and self-granting *Dasein*. But the crucial difference that Derrida produces is a simultaneous retention of a phenomenology of consciousness and its straying in the process of linguistic representation. But just as being is disclosed through a sequence of exterior points in space and time, linguistic representation of such a sequence generates 'signs' that disclose this dynamic of 'spacing' and 'timing'. Habermas makes his basic critique of Derrida in dirempting language in such a process of writing that resists the communication of meanings showed by its users and instead curtailing it to generate an interminable sequence of signs. The movement of such signs moves in a disparate occultation of already established functions of speech and writing into a structure of difference in which the sign differs from itself not only by its 'spacing and 'timing', but by defamiliarising itself from all possible reference. Habermas contends that Derrida's adoption of such a method is 'mystic' as it claims to reveal what lies behind our attribution of sense and meaning and what remains as a 'transcendental unconditioned' behind the structure of thought, meaning and communication. In Habermas' opinion, Derrida's writing calls forth all the interpretations of the 'traces' and the more unfamiliar they become, the more they renew the mystical concept of tradition as an event, delayed event and revelation.

Such a mystic mood, Habermas points out, is all intended to experience an 'unbounded claim of what is outside the everyday', but it is self-stultifying as the deconstructive enterprise produces refuse heaps of interpretations in order to get at the buried foundations of what is held commonly, and it never settles with what it gets because it cannot accept those supposedly 'distorted' meanings. This is a self-stultifying methodological tract. Habermas cites the 'tract' like primacy of 'rhetoric' over 'logic' and the notion of a generalised context that submerges all specific 'text'. This is how Derrida develops another history of being, encoded into texts with the more disastrous consequence of foregrounding the 'ontic', so that everything can be relegated to the ontologically unconditioned context to *arachi-writing*. This movement leads 'back into the ontology of being' that Heidegger, Nietzche and Derrida wanted to overcome.[14] This rise of a 'general context' is conterminous with the notion of a universal 'text', which, in Habermas' apt characterisation, lacks all performative function, just as a 'promise' in its quoted form.[15] Derrida's philosophical instrument of such a 'universal text', for Habermas, puts into question the very possibility of having various contexts of meaning and is involved in a performative contradiction. Habermas feels that one cannot put into question one's 'context' of affirmation by a generalised inclusion of all such contexts into a meta-context that does not admit a specific context.

So, one has to retain distinctions of 'genres', if one is to succeed in communicating a definite thematic or text, that is one has to uphold a 'context' in order to make oneself intelligible. Habermas criticises Derrida for putting into question the very context of meaning and rational argumentation. In his words:

> For Derrida, the linguistically mediated processes within the world are embedded in a world constituting context that prejudices everything; they are fatalistically delivered upto the unmanageable happening of text production, overwhelmed by the poetic-creative transformation of a background designed by arch writing, and condemned to be provincial.[16]

This reification of the function of language produces even graver consequences, as it undermines the validity basis of the action of understanding and relegates it behind the world creating capacity of language. Derrida accomplishes this by aestheticising language, produced with the two-fold denial of the proper sense of the world creating capacity of language. This involves aestheticisation of the language that produces the two-fold denial of the proper sense of the 'normal' and 'poetic' discourse.

This critique by Habermas gets a critical response as Derrida says:

> (...) In a pragmatically determined situation in which (...) 'truth' is set forth (the questioning of the possibility of truth, etc., and the discourse attuned to that questioning?) must submit (...) to the norms of the context that require one to prove, to demonstrate, to proceed correctly, to conform to the rules of language and to a great number of other social, ethical, political-institutional rules, etc.[17]

But the crux question that Derrida raises is that by accepting the rules of a context, can we draw a necessary normative formulation of the stability of that context and determine all the linguistic, social, ethical, political conclusions? What is more important for Derrida is the condition of possibility of such a context and the built-in non-identity in the norms of intelligibility drawn from/of such a context. This is formulated by Derrida in the notion of 'double writing', which must inevitably partition itself along two sides of a limit,[18] that is it must follow the rules of that which has given rise to such a discourse. Therefore, it participates in a discourse and externalises the perspective of a participant in a discourse and produces the external perspective of what makes the discourse possible. Deconstruction, in that sense, is a simultaneous decoding of the participation in the discourse as well as an encoding of what made the discourse. Deconstruction plays one such aspect against the other in order to explore the opening of 'inside' to the 'outside'; and closing of 'outside' to the 'inside'. This methodical operation of deconstruction unravels those norms of communication that go into making the very structure of language employed in a particular discourse. One can see the implications of such a restitution of norms of communication in terms of the structural aspects of language in Derrida's notion of *différance*, which differs in the meaning of a term used in a previous context to a newer context, making meaning all the more context dependent. Habermas' notion of 'criticisable validity claims' deciphered in a process of communication comes through such Derridean 'deferral'. A claim becomes criticisable only when it defers from its own meaning. Criticisability, therefore, implies an interruption from another context, which is precisely the deferral of the previous context of the claim. Further a criticisable validity claim yields place to a claim different from it. Such possibilities of deferral-difference emanates not as a transcendental condition of the possibility of the criteria of validity claims, but as a practical possibility in the process of communication. Therefore, such construction accomplishes the task of an immanent critique of validity claims that arise from differentiated spheres of society by exploring the possibility of criticising them from one context within the same sphere. But the crucial difference with Habermas comes in Derrida's deconstructive demonstration of the impossibility of arriving at those transcendental conditions of possibility that makes validity claims iterable in various contexts. Hence, Derridean deconstruction exposes the elusiveness of deriving the rules and norms of discourse that operate as transcendental conditions of the possibility of a discourse. Such transcendental conditions of the possibility of discourse are not same as the normative structure of the life-world, and hence, Habermas' claim of recuperation of the normative structure of the life-world in language sounds more like a resuscitation of a transcendental set of norms, which is simply irrecoverable in the discourse constituted by language. For Habermas, norms or rules of discourse are not constituted by language, but are socially created to make validity claims in the process of communication. For Derrida, such a distinction between norms or rules and the discourse is only arbitrary, because the norms or rules of discourse can only be related to the norms or rules of society, not in one isomorphic way, but by way of difference.

Therefore what follows from Habermas' critique of Rorty and Derrida can be put simply in this way:

> (1) In the case of Rorty, the lack of any transcendental basis for agreement takes away the substances from Rorty's project of community-centred agreement, and (2) in the case of Derrida, the unconditioned basis of particular contextual claims get attenuated into an endless hermeneutic deferral.

This Habermasian critique has serious epistemic implications in terms of re-affirmation of the unconditioned basis of all knowledge claims, which, for him, is the normative aspect of such claims. He combines the unconditioned basis of knowledge-claims bearing an identity with the basis of the normative structure of society. Rorty's response to such a critique and its implications re-assert the nature of an already existing circularity between knowledge claim and belief, language and shared norms, all cohering in a responsible manner. This implies that any theory about holding of knowledge, norm, belief, etc., cannot single them out and provide a linear explanation without taking into account the already existing coherence between them. Derrida's critique of validity claims in terms of exploration of the possibility of the context signifies that no normative description can provide a sufficient explanation for agreement or disagreement in communication. Even though a theory of communication can be construed upon mutually agreed linguistic usage, such a theory is bound to fail in accounting for the multiple possibilities of meaning and the instability of context in which these meanings are produced.

To sum up, this open-ended debate between the modernist and the postmodernist epistemic perspective turns out to be a debate between two basic epistemic premises:

(1) Knowledge should have universal validity and such a notion of validity is derived from the transcendental conditions of knowledge.

(2) Knowledge can have only contextual relevance and contexts are never stable. Such contexts only acquire a relative stability to give a specific meaning, while such meanings themselves are open to possibilities of intervention and change.

These two premises conflict with each other in terms of the determination of a stable meaning of knowledge claims. For a modernist like Habermas, such stability is normative in character, while for Rorty and Derrida, no knowledge claim can give rise to a fixed normative conclusion and it can only give rise to an ongoing discourse of ever-altering meaning.

A Postmodernist Critique of 'Modern' Habermas by Rorty and Derrida's Critique of Habermas

Rorty and Derrida independently develop a critique of Habermas' derivation of the transcendental-pragmatic 'norm' of argumentation from the nature of validity of the knowledge claims involved in the cognitive, moral and aesthetic spheres of life. For Rorty, derivation of the normative procedure from knowledge claims would be a functionalist enterprise, as at the level of social theory, it establishes 'validity' based upon such normative procedure. For Derrida, such a derivation would be an exercise in predetermination of the 'context' and also a metaphysical 'closure' that suppresses the whole process of difference in the process of communication. For Rorty, Habermas' separation of 'normative' as the basis for the 'social' is a form of dualism between world and social and what Habermas does is an inverse derivation of those social norms from linguistic to practical and not the other way round. For Rorty, both these ways would mean continuation of the goal of hermeneutics. Further, at the level of social theory it gives a universalisable status to norms and draws a naturalised equivalence to the operation of rationality. This is how Habermas erects a 'foundational' theory of society. For Derrida, Habermas' whole project of communicative action is an under-determination of various context of speech and action, which turns language into a mere 'tool' of rationality. For both Rorty and Derrida, derivation of norms is a matter of taking 'decisions'. Decisions are an act of choice just as much as they are an act of opening what has already come through, a matter of meeting the truth to which one has to be responsible. In choosing between plurality of norms, a postmodern society or an individual necessarily undertakes an operation of sharing with an other what she decides to perform.[19]

To sort out the issues, let me briefly sum up the Rortyean critique of Habermas a la a critique of some of the basic presuppositions of modernist epistemology. Rorty's reading of Habermas tries to ease him out of the bracketing of every social action in terms of a coherent rule-following moral order by way of historicising the acceptability dimension of Habermas' claim. In doing so, Rorty tried to read the postmodern inklings in Habermas' thoughts by way of locating, only negatively, his effort at combining a rationality of science with that of primacy of 'reason' in the modern social order, which he interprets more clearly by citing Habermas' agreement with Hegel in the 'need for unification' in order to 'regenerate the unifying power of religion in the medium of reason'.[20] Rorty combines these two aspects of Habermas' explanation: rationality of science with the unifying capacity of reason, in which Rorty sees 'unity' as a hidden telos in Habermas' social theory. In Rorty's understanding, "This is an old Kantian problematique that puts the human subject in the universalisable character of the communication community".[21] Even though such a coherence between the human subject, reason and communication emanates from 'Kant's stubborn differentiation'[22], Rorty will still grant that Habermas' notion of the 'communication community' operates in a quite plausible way of making its presence felt in liberal communities that are inclusive and open by nature. But Rorty reminds us of Habermas' concern for a 'de-differentiating' effect of belonging to such a community, as it fails to give direction to the sense of belonging in a 'constitutive' sense. Rorty finds it unnecessary to have such a constitutive sense through impersonal normative qualification, as this will produce an 'alienating effect' on members of the society quite in the way the 'philosophy of subject' had intended. Rorty especially cites Habermas' emphasis on validity claims, which could be employed 'in the case of repression and emancipation of conscious', the shared intersubjective consciousness for which Habermas stands. For Rorty, such an emphasis on validity is nothing but a reiteration of the 'philosophy of subject' that only gives rise to a historicist narrative, which turns into a metanarrative when it aims at unity of the differentiated spheres of life by way of inserting an artistic urge to do so, which in itself is an art that represents the atomised individual. Rorty's caution to this kind of an 'aesthetic of the beautiful' is that it can never 'present the fact that the unrepresentable exists.' Rorty's notion of sublime represents the unrepresented, instead of an already formed subject' or 'community' or a form of differentiated life, in which everybody can share their hopes and despairs. Rorty contends that the possibility of sharing life by finding 'beautiful ways of harmonising interest' does not come in conflict with the quest of the sublime in the way the modern quest for the beautiful debunks the sublime for the sake of representation. Rather, the quest for the sublime and the quest for the beautiful go together, one giving rise to a postmodernist form of 'intellectual', life and the other giving rise to a postmodernist form of 'social life'. Seemingly, Rorty has agreed with Habermas on the quest for harmonising social life by having a 'communication community', but differs in respect of his advocacy of a normatively regulated social order.

Habermas' obvious reply to such Rortyean critique would be a critique of Rorty's utopian liberalism, which tries to erect this edifice without any commonly shared rationality. Further, Habermas would debunk Rorty's dualism between 'sublime' and 'beauty' as a postmodern 'de-differentiation', as the linking up of the two would give rise to historical communities who struggle for changing an order.

Derrida's Critique of Habermas and Habermas' Response

Derrida's critique of Habermas would follow his critique of Austin, as Habermas merely re-interpreted the Austinian notion of 'performative utterance' in terms of transcendental-pragmatic presuppositions of universalisable validity claims. Derrida's critique of Austin for demanding a permanent value for the 'context' and for the claim of an 'intentional meaning' is relevant in a similar adaptation of Habermas in his theory of 'communicative action'. Apart from this, Derrida's general critique of the notion of communication would be the aforementioned critique of Austin in order to flash out the features of a Derridean critique.

Derrida's critique of the notion of 'communication' stems from his idea of a differential structure of writing that relates an absent addressee to here and now contexts, which may not signify a stable, fixed and determined circumstance. Derrida extrapolates this notion of writing in the analysis of utterances that are performative. It results in the notion that every performative utterance follows a model of 'citation', which is cited in necessary contexts and as such, citation determines its 'iteration' and not an exterior context determining citation of a statement. Derrida circumscribes this notion of citation within the notion of writing, in order to show that the possibility of iteration, as in the case of written signs also inhabits the spoken word and this results in a process of the repeatability of words in every utterance of itself. But with every utterance, the repeatable words produce a structure of difference and this structure in every repetition further becomes an act of citation.

As context will change in every repetition, previously acquired meaning will undergo a process of repetition to produce various meanings in various contexts. Derrida gives an example of citation of the same poem or song, assuming various 'meanings' in various contexts. What Derrida contends is the difference of 'intentionality', which leads to the failure of a citeable statement to mean identically the same in different contexts.

This whole critique of Derrida could be juxtaposed in Habermas' notion of communicative reason. This juxtaposition would open up a close conception of communication that is conceived in terms of the sharing of commonly understandable meanings of 'shared intentionality' in terms of reference. The first effect of this is an exposure of the idealising conditions of communication in terms of absence of an addressee, i.e. a stable context of meaning. This opens up a renewed notion of communication in which Derrida's metaphoric description of an *envois* or postal message presents how linguistic expressions, utterances, talk, etc., are directed to an 'other' who receives it, and how it lies between the sender and the receiver, that is, one who utters and one who responds.[23] The question that arises here is, Does Derrida deny the communication of the same sense which the utterer intended the listener to receive? Derrida's approach is to answer this question with another question: From where does the speaker derive the command of communicating the same sense as she intended? If the answer to this question is that it is derived from 'shared conventions', then Derrida would say that the assumption of shared context and convention is a pre-determination, contrary to which the context of the speaker and hearer is re-created in the process of communication, despite their sharing of a common code of meaning. The context is re-created in the process of hearing and responding, that is in the process of exchanging. In a direct address to a person, such an exchange originates and returns to itself, but an address returns to itself only by changing hands. So, Derrida foregrounds his thesis that linguistic communication is a form of exchange that puts speaker and hearer in a place of sharing, but the act of sharing is a process of switching over the context of utterance into a new context and so on.

The second effect of the critique is that what arises as moments of agreement and disagreement stems out of common and conventional meaning, but this is nothing but a play of difference, as what is agreed upon is just a matter of norm or convention and it will be different, given the possibility that within the same conventions, contextual variations will produce difference. Agreement further defers the meaning to different possible contexts, while it makes possible the employment of the same speech-acts with a different meaning. What Derrida points out is that the possibility of agreement is conditioned by conventions and context, while linguistic expression itself can exceed such conditions and produce a different meaning altogether by producing a different condition of communication. It means that the possible agreement could be deferred to a number of in-determinable contexts that would make communication in-terminable between addresses.

The third effect will combine both the first and the second, that is a combination for change of context in the exchange between participants in linguistic communication. This plus deferring of meaning through iteration of speech-acts produce the third effect of impossibility of deriving fixed norms of communication. Such a derivation of universal norms of communication is impossible precisely because change of context and the possibility of iteration imply an absence of addressees and, thereby, those who participate in the process of exchange merely assume them to be subjects of an exchange and assume a definite agreement on meaning. Such an assumption is meant only for facilitating an exchange and not for closing the exchange into certain norms and conventions between the participants. Therefore, from a Derridean perspective, what

Habermas derives as norms of rational argumentation is an extrapolation of the assumed stability of the context of communication into a general context of reason. Looked from another perspective, norms of argumentation are interpolated into communicative exchanges by Habermas in order to give a rational theory of communication. Habermas' claim that communication must involve universalisable rationality and normative structure could very well be disputed by the simple fact that rationality structures cannot be identified with culturally based norms of intelligibility. Further, Habermas' distinction between undistorted and distorted communication based upon a universalisable condition of shared rationality appeals to a transcendental intersubjective agreement on rules of reason, which are conceived as transcendental conditions of possibility of communication. From a Derridean point of view, such transcendental conditions of the possibility of discourse can neither define rationality nor be derived from rationality. Supposing it is done, it would merely delimit the possibility of discourse and participation in that. But the act of communication through the discourse must switch one from one context to another and become iterable.[24] Derrida exposes the transcendental naivete of such a view as Habermas proposed in his theory of communicative action.

On the other hand, Derrida theorises the multi-possibilities involved in communication in 'apocalyptic' theses when he affirms, 'addresses without message and without destination, without sender or decidable addressee'. What Derrida contends here is the iteration of signs in linguistic communication that surpasses the fixed determination of subjectivities and sends it over to more iteration. Habermas' notion of 'distorted communication' can ironically be conceived here in Derrida's critique of fixed subjectivities engaged in communication and Habermas' binding of such subjectives within fixed rules of reason.

Habermas' reply to such a critique by Derrida would consist in re-iterating the need for transcendence that is more full of content and meaningful than the purely formal transcendence from within[25] to which we are exposed by the force of validity claims, which he advocates in his theory of communicative action. With greater force of conviction, Habermas asserts.

> The inevitable canalisation of everyday life in political communication also poses a danger for the semantic potential on which such communication must draw (...). Even that moment of unconditionality, which is stubbornly expressed by the transcendence of validity claims of everyday communication, is not sufficient. Another kind of transcendence is disclosed in the undiffused force (...) which the critical appropriation of identity-forming religious traditions, and yet another in the negativity of modern (...). The trivial must be allowed to shatter against the sheerly alien, abyssal, uncanny (...) which resists assimilation of what is already understood, although no privilege can now install itself behind it.[26]

Such problematisation of the unconditionality of the transcendental norms of validity of argumentation, communication and rationality is Habermas' tacit allusion to those forms of communication which lie beyond his binary opposition between distorted and undistorted forms of communication and which are trivial, uncanny and resist assimilation with the norms of ordinary communication. What Derrida characterises is the difference of linguistic communication as an affirmation of the decentred subjectivity through iterability that subverts the stable context of meaning and its condition of possibility. Further, he advocates an open field of communication to an unlimited play of signifiers, which has been trivially re-enacted in Habermas' tribute to the uncanny power of the religious language within modernity that addresses transcendence. This is what has remained a key problematique of Derridean deconstruction, which opens up space for an 'experience of the impossible', which presupposes 'hospitality without reserve' towards the singularity of the event. This is what Derrida characterises as apocalyptic or messianic. This is what he further calls a quasi-theory of undecidability?. So, deconstruction becomes an exploration of as many instants of undecidability as time itself. It always tends to say that only undecidability is permanent. The undecidability proceeds, follows and permeates the decision, that is the undecidability is first, last and always, but that decisions must be made and indecisions broken. What this shows is the secret of impossibility that goes along with every condition of possibility and which remains as the other side of any affirmation of possibility.

To sum up, Rorty and Derrida's critique of Habermas points out the impossibility of deriving a structure of rationality that regulates both society and human communication; Habermas' critique of Rorty and Derrida points out the failure of their stances in rising above mere contextual possibilities without even giving it a definitive meaning. In terms of its interpretive implication, Rorty's and Derrida's critique of Habermas explain why Habermas has fallen into a transcendental fold that fails to reconcile the experience of the uncanny. Habermas' critique of Rorty and Derrida brings back the charge of aestheticisation of meaning and language to the extent that it becomes ineffective in communicating any meaning.

Notes

1. Jurgen Habermas, "Themes in Postmetaphysical Thinking" in *PMT*, p.
2. *TCA*, Vol. II, p. 137.
3. Jurgen Habermas, "Philosophy as Stand-in and Interpreter" in *MCCA*, pp. 1-22, see p. 10.
4. *MCCA*, pp. 13-17.
5. Jurgen Habermas, "Questions and Counter Questions", *Praxis International* 4 (1984), pp. 229-249. See p. 234.
6. *PDM*, p. 231.
7. *PDM*, p. 231.
8. *ORT*, p. 83.

9. *ORT*, p. 144.
10. *ORT*, pp. 145-46.
11. R. Bernstein, ed. *Habermas and Modernity*, MIT Press, Cambridge, 1999, pp, 167-75.
12. T. McCarthy, "Ironist Theory as a Vocation: A Response to Rorty's Reply", *Critical Inquiry*, 16(1990), pp. 644-655, see pp. 644-45.
13. *PMT*, p. 51.
14. *PDM*, p. 192.
15. *PDM*, p. 194.
16. *PDM*, p. 206.
17. Jacques Derrida, *LI*, pp. 150-1.
18. Jacques Derrida, *LI*, p. 152.
19. Chantal Mouffe, ed., *Deconstruction and Pragmatism*, Routledge, 1996, p. 85.
20. *EHO*, p. 169.
21. *EHO*, p. 170.
22. *EHO*, p. 170.
23. *TCA*, Vol. I, pp. 330-31.
24. Jacques Derrida, "Double Session' in *D*, pp. 246, "Of An Apocalyptic Tone Recently Adopted in Philosophy", trans., John P. Peavey Jr. *Semeia*, 23, 1982.
25. *PMT*, p. 51.
26. *FN*, p. 377.

VI

Critical Polemics – II: Postmodernism's Inner Subversions

*Rorty and Derrida in Crossing****

Rorty's radical abandonment of epistemology in favour of concrete social practices and Derrida's critique of an uncontaminated existence of a liberal community run at cross-purposes. While Rorty goes towards critical reconstruction of a liberal community, Derrida drifts towards a radicalisation of the already existing practices of constructing the world and the social order. Rorty's goal is to accomplish a liberal community that includes the greatest possible plurality, specificity and sensitivity to identity with others. Derrida's goal is to critically question all such modes of settled practices and rests upon an avenue to break through existing social and political practices. From such divergent perspectives, the postmodern image of human life assumes a simultaneous persistence and dissipation of its established mores, dancing at its own funeral and re-christening its own failings to emerge into new melodies. Such a conflicting and destabilising field of forces keeps breaking and re-constituting postmodern images. Neither Rorty nor Derrida can contribute a singular explanation that transcends the ways of the world, instead their contributions in terms of re-interpretation and critique set a particular tone in philosophy, the appropriation of which generates a wide-ranging debate on the very characteristics of the postmodern conceptualisation. The purpose of this chapter is to first identify the directions in which Rorty and Derrida come together in some kind of coincidence and then to elaborate upon those coincidences through Rorty's critique of Derrida and vice versa. The chapter draws upon such critique and counter-critique in order to identify the crossroads of postmodernism.

Coincidences between Rorty and Derrida

The coincidences between Rorty and Derrida come through in their abandonment of the metaphysical circle of reason and acceptance of a discourse-centred idea of reason. But such coincidence goes in *two* different directions: Rorty carries out his critique of metaphysics to the extent that it does not serve the interests of the community (in the liberal postmodern sense), while Derrida carries it out in order to bring out the 'claim' of any discourse. Thus, Rorty turns ethnocentric, while Derrida gives rise to a more global critical practice with his supposedly neutral method of deconstruction by way of exposing the possibilities of going beyond what a specific configuration of discourse(s) aims at. This difference between Rorty and Derrida sustains its gravity in their mutual criticism and recognition of each other's points, which produce a critical distance. Rorty diagnoses two mutually countervailing aspects in the practice of deconstruction: one, it wins over the tendencies to fall back on metaphysical and epistemic determinations, and two, it turns against itself by undermining its critical spirit in its quest for reaching at those transcendental conditions that regulate a field of discourse. Derrida merely locates a streak of romantic hangover in Rorty's understanding of him. On the other hand Derrida would prescribe 'interminability' in one's deciphering of critical meanings in whatever has acquired a stable meaning. To chart out the terrain of this critique and counter–critique between Rorty and Derrida, I shall first delineate Rorty's critique of Derrida and then proceed to look into Derrida's possible response and later to Derrida's critique of Rorty's liberal pragmatism and Rorty's possible response. I shall thus derive epistemologically significant critique that can be arrived at from this whole exercise.

Rorty's Critique of Derrida

Rorty begins his critique of Derrida by charging him of a general undifferentiated 'textualism' that goes into the nitty-gritty of how the 'text' is produced and how the texts lean on metaphysical-conceptual opposition. Rorty maintains a double stance on such an idea of undifferentiated externalism by suggesting that it should be promoted to the extent that it subverts the artificial distinctions between genres of writing and opens up 'literary' and poetic' moments in various areas of our culture. It should be discouraged to the extent that it aims at the philosophical project of overcoming onto-theological tradition. So far as promotion is concerned, Rorty appropriates deconstruction in the service of liberalism. Such a strategy would bring deconstruction onto a level playing field with Rorty's pragmatism or liberalism. Contrary to Derrida's confinement within the conceptual oppositions produced within the text, Rorty's retention of an exterior criterion of social practice is a way of grounding such texts. Epistemically, Derrida's metaphysical quests for the search of opposition are contrasted by Rorty's search for answers to concrete social questions and the two distinct criteria play off each other. Rorty combines such a contrast with his flare for social practices in exploring a deconstructive pragmatic possibility in the understanding of language.

Rorty locates the attempt to turn ordinary linguistic practice into a domain of settling metaphysical issues, like whether there is some one substance, or whether the way the world is must count in our ascription of truth-value to language. He relates such metaphysical criteria to the size of certain pseudo-notions like verifiability and intelligibility that philosophical vocabulary aims to acquire:

> Not only must a philosophical vocabulary be total in the sense that anything literally or metaphorically sayable in other vocabulary can be literally said in it, but it must speak of itself with the same 'assumed legibility" as it does of everything else.[1]

Precisely, Rorty considers 'language' as a field of metaphorical meanings which is more literary than literal in its nature. What is meant in such characterisation is that language surpasses philosophy's search for one all-inclusive vocabulary that can give rise to certain rules of meaning in relation to other vocabularies. Rorty makes a critical juxtaposition between philosophy's dream (pace Derrida)[2] for such a vocabulary with ordinary linguistic practice and the possibility of uses of multiple vocabularies in various modes of writing. The juxtaposition results in a notion of irreducibility of such variety of vocabularies into one another.[3] This brings together two consequences: one, vocabularies need not be deconstructed in order to unpack the hidden metaphysical basis of any kind of vocabulary, and two, one kind of vocabulary can be replaced with another in cases when one finds them insufficient and anomalous.[4] Rorty relates this play of vocabularies in crediting Derrida with opening up closed vocabularies of philosophy. He credits Derrida with opening up the philosophical texts to other texts, which lie in a weave of difference of forces in the wider field of language. Such a possibility of a wider field of differences envisages a total transformation of a culture marked by self-conscious interminability, self-conscious openness and self-conscious lack of philosophical closure. This is simultaneously an opening of the philosophical, metaphysical and epistemological texts to something non-philosophical—one can call it a self-conscious blurring of distinctions between philosophy and non-philosophy, which makes one act from outside the margins of philosophy. But such an opening is fraught with the dilemma of either retaining philosophy or abandoning it totally, similar to Nietzsche and Heidegger's attempts to overcome the metaphysics of being, which forced them either in the direction of setting with eternal return or to name of the being which remains in-describable within philosophy. But such eternal return or name of the being is what they intended to overcome. So Derrida takes recourse to those metaphors that indicate such an overcoming and all those metaphors are built by him around writing so that this time, there is no metaphysical return to 'being'. Such a metaphoric adaptation of a philosophical project brings into language the possibility of removing all traces or grounds for truth or a unified theory of knowledge; it brings into the picture a stream of unconnected sentences, vocabularies and metaphors carrying no inferential relation between them. Such a re-interpretation of writing presents a two-horned dilemma: on the one hand, it is a writing without a fixed telos or architecture, and on the other, such a writing can claim the states of a metavocabulary that can explain all other possible vocabularies.[5] What Rorty explains here is the epistemic dilemma of deconstruction: going transcendental undermines the actually available texts, while remaining with texts without a fixed metaphysical or teleological logos means an open and non-inferential mode of representation. Rorty points out that the dilemma goes deeper in the whole terrain of Derridean deconstruction. Derridean claims like (1) production of several languages and several texts and (2) moments of difference[6] as the common root of all conceptual resources reconfigures the dilemma that (1) presents the possibility of the opening up of the text, and (2) speaks of a philosophical process through which concepts in language[7] acquire their functions. Both the claims taken together present two different and mutually counterposing concerns; one trying to open up texts to other texts and the other trying to identify the common root of conceptual opposition as a depth mechanism. Rorty sees the possibility of an opening in the first that goes quite well with his project of inventing newer vocabularies, while the search for a ground of opposition in the second remains as a mark of denying the liberal possibility of multiplicity of genres and cultures, a kind of one versus many that such a search generates. In Rorty's words:

> What pragmatists find most foreign in Derrida is his suspicion of empiricism and naturalism—his assumption that these are forms of metaphysics, rather than replacements for metaphysics. To put it in another way; they cannot understand why Derrida wants to sound transcendental, why he persists in taking the project of finding conditions of possibility seriously. So, when pragmatists are told by 'deconstructionists' that Derrida has 'demonstrated' that Y, the condition of possibility of X, is also the condition of impossibility of X, they feel that this is an unnecessary flaunting way of putting across a point which could be put a lot more simply: viz, that you cannot use the word A without being able to use the word B and vice versa, even though nothing can be both an A and B.[8]

Rorty's nominalist-pragmatist way of putting things concerns itself not with the 'discourse of philosophy, but with the useful application of vocabularies stemming out of such discourse. Such useful application of vocabularies assumes a critical dimension in Rorty's critique of 'conditions of possibility', which are non-causal conditions, yet they are misleading ways of making the point that a certain set of terms cannot be used by people who are incapable of using another set. So Rorty asks the question, how can one grasp the conditions of all possible contexts? The question takes into account the claim made by some professed Derrideans like de Man and Christopher Norris, who have read Derrida either in terms of nihilating all possible meaning by a transvaluational idiom or in terms of an a priori critique of the power and limits of texts.[10] In all such readings, Derrida's deconstruction is identified as a transcendental project, as a project of reaching the grounds of any discourse or concept, but Rorty adds a further dimension to the problematic nature of this project by asking the question,

> Within what language are we to lay out arguments demonstrating (or even just making plausible) that we have correctly identified these conditions?[11]

Rorty considers these questions a major Achilles' heel in the transcendental project because it restricts the context of use of language, and once it is restricted in this way, it turns regressive in borrowing expressions from what it conditions as 'context'. But the transcendental project elevates that borrowed language for various contexts. This means a counterproductive situation in which contexts are already determined by the metalanguage, which makes no sense in talking about various linguistic usages in various contexts. Rorty aptly cites how Gasche reads in Derrida the Hegelian philosophy of reflection because he found out the conditions of possibility that determine the conceptual relationship. Concepts in such a reading of Derrida are always 'cracked and fissured' by the trace of its opposites. So, Rorty concludes that:

> The best we nominalists can do with such claims is to construe them by saying that one can always make old language look (...) by thinking up a better one—replace an old tool with a new one by using an old word in a new way (e.g. as a privilege rather than the derivative term of a contrast), or by replacing it with a new word. But this need for replacement is ours, not the concept's. It does not go to pieces, rather we set it aside and replace it with something else.[12]

Rorty effectively follows this kind of renewal, replacement and re-creation by citing two major readings of Derrida by some of his great disciples like Paul de Man and Hillis Miller. Rorty cities how de Man, following Derridean deconstruction, considered 'poetic language' as naming 'the presence of a nothingness',[13] a language that represents an abyss created from deconstruction of the subject and knowledge. Such a de Manian interpretation of language[14] hinges upon a contrast with the phenomenal world and the way it acts upon human subjectivity. Such a contrast makes language the voice of a dark god, who speaks in a literary language and de Man considers a writing like 'literature' as giving a sense of 'no exit' from the 'condition that is felt to be unbearable',[15] an experience of the void and the abyss that cannot be known, but only 'named with ever-renewed understanding'.[16] This is what jibes well with ready-made understanding of Derridean claims like the following:

> The sign represents the present in absence. The sign in this use is deferred presence.[17]

This is what Rorty identifies with 'hypostatisation of language' in ways such as those with which Hillis Miller characterises language:

> Language promises, but what it promises is itself. The promises it can never keep. It is this fact of language, a necessity beyond the control of any user of language, which makes things happen as they do happen in the material world of history.[18]

Rorty calls such an understanding of language as hypostatisation as it images language as a field of permanent absence and it preserves de Manian contrast with the phenomenal world in the form of drawing an equivalence so abstract that it gives language the role of 'showing up' certain fictional or poetic events, which are imaginary and yet retains a law-like worldly correspondence between such imaginary and fictional events. Such a deliberate tie-up between phenomenal world and language as Rorty conceives it is a result of 'trying to bring everything together—one's most private emotional needs and one's public responsibilities'.[19] Rorty further interprets this abyssal effect of deconstruction in pragmatic terms and sees a mechanism of self-eschewment and guilt consciousness in such attenuation of language into an 'uncontrolled' espousing of life through a fission of signs. In Rorty's lens, such a worshipping of a hypostatised form of language is simultaneously a mark of ironising the world, a perennial quality of intellectuals who also want to redeem their 'selves' from such voids and re-construct it in newer vocabularies. Further hypostatisation bears a sense of 'guilt' in so far as the intellectuals cannot create their own project of self-invention for the needs of those who are less capable of re-description and re-invention.[20]

The question that arises here is whether Rorty's nominalist and liberal interpretation of deconstruction gets the better of the dilemma between 'transcendence' and 'opening', or it merely replicates it in a different way. At least Rorty's pragmatic truck with the deconstructive notion of 'openness' in terms of an ability 'to substitute sensible signs with other signs'[21] reinstates the deconstructive dilemma in terms of 'private perfection' and 'public responsibility'. His nominalist notion of re-description remains meaningful in the realms of the private. Rorty's dismissal of Derrida's transcendental project as a circumvention of the play of language and, hence, restrictive of the possibility of re-description revives Derrida's own dilemma between inside and outside, impossible and possible. Still, Derrida's exegesis retains a deconstructive leeway to the dilemma as Simon Critchley's counterbalancing question reflects:

> Whether Rorty's pragmatism is in fact pragmatist all the way down, or whether its commitment to liberation, in terms of a non-relativisable claim about the susceptibility of human beings to suffering and the need to minimise cruelty transgresses the limits of Rorty's pragmatism.[22]

Derrida's Defence of the Transcendental Project and his Consequent Critique of Rorty

From a Derridean point of view, the question that arises is whether Derrida would agree to Rorty's understanding of his search for 'conditions of possibility of context, meaning and writing'. Especially Rorty's debunking of such conditions of possibility as something contrary to the possibility of openness or newness necessitates an answer to the question formulated above. In responding to the question, one has to locate the response in the Derridean notion of general economy of difference, which is a structural principle that governs the structure of writing in general. For Derrida, writing is a process of chaining together signs that follow a rule of differing and deferring, differing from itself as well as other signs and deferring its presence altogether. Such a structure of difference suspends the presence of signs altogether. Such a structure of difference never gives the full presence of signs to itself; rather, it is a process in which signs appear only to erase themselves in traces. Such traces produce the always moving structure of writing, which is without a fixed locus, but stretched along a field, heterogeneous in character. Derrida's questions of transcendental conditions of possibility need to be contextualised in his structure of writing called difference. This is Derrida's way of posing the question in its relation to writing and in its possibility of breaking through, that is in a simultaneous relation of belonging and not-belonging. This takes us to the Derridean interpretation of transcendence, which is a real structure like economic, historical, etc., all of which becomes real in an interpretive move. The interpretive move is an attempt to arrive at a certain stable meaning for some kind of activities, but what lurks through such a move is the Derridean question, What are the conditions of possibility of such structures? Another question that crops up through an act of interpretation is, Are the conditions or limits of a context determinable? These two structures of writing are present only by closing their limits, an enclosure that opens up at the limits. So, its 'presence' lies at the 'limit', while it is open and wide at its limit. Derrida's search for conditions of possibility is a question that emanantes from the limits of the context, namely can such limits determine themselves totally or are they just an extraction from the world or just a way of grounding in the world? Derrida's answer that conditions of possibility include those items that are excluded by the context and that hence, context produces an inside containing what is conceived from within it and produces an outside that includes all that are excluded. Conditions of possibility dissolve this line between inside and outside and it simultaneously gives rise to a possibility of having a context. At the same time, the Derridean answer to Rorty's paraphrasing of conditions of possibility can be reformulated in this way: It is not to use the word 'B', which is no guarantee to be able to use the word 'A'. What this means is that the 'condition of possibility' is a derivation to know that other possibilities remain, when one thing is made possible. Translated in pragmatic terms, it is not merely to use signs, but it is also the capacity to relate signs with contexts of real life that deconstruction purports to in its paradigm statement, 'nothing outside the text'.[23] Rorty approves of such an approach in his notion of recontextualisation which advocates relations between various texts.

Derrida himself defines his transcendental enterprise because asking for the transcendental condition of possibility is not just confronting empiricism, positivism and psychologism, but reaching into an area that makes an event both possible and impossible. This is an area that Derrida articulates as a function that defines possibility as a function of impossibility, that is defining possibility as its impossibility, which further signifies the deconstructive move to go beyond the possible. Derrida terms this position on transcendentality as 'quasi-transcendental' as it is neither 'a bland approval of possibility nor a flat talk about impossibility'[24], rather it is contrapuntal in the sense that possibility breaks through the impossibility and vice versa. This is transcendental only in a reflective sense, while in actual terms, it is the possibility of the condition of possibility.[25] Derrida calls this position highly unorthodox and distinguishes it from the traditional Kantian-Husserlian notion of the transcendental which takes only a grasp upon the realm of possible, but, claims that the grasp is total.

A subtler critique of Rorty is generated in Derrida's defence of the transcendental project. He also counter-questions Rorty's objections to the conditions of possibility by pointing out:

> How is that something 'X', which does not have a stable meaning or reference, becomes indispensable in certain finite, but open, context during a certain period of time, for a certain number of actors?[26]

Derrida answers this question in the context of a supposed relationship between deconstruction and pragmatism, Rorty supposes so. The relationship between the two is of such a kind that they are disentangled in such a way that there can be an articulation of similar purpose without a common shared basis. Assuming its nominalist face, Rorty's pragmatism tries to handle the resources of deconstruction, but finds it circumventing the beliefs of liberal democracy. Deconstruction, on the other hand, takes a pragmatic cue, which is a form of dispelling closure in a culture such that it can absorb new trends in it. With this lack of fit between deconstruction's commitment to contain the condition of possibility and pragmatism's non-committal webs of beliefs, manifest in understanding how decisions are taken and in what ways, Rorty's immediate answer is that the way things are or 'the way it is good in the belief of the community' reduces the scope of decidability in choosing from a set of givens.[27] But this way of determination of 'the way things are' or 'the way it is good in the belief of the community' leaves open the relationship between the human subjects, choices and decisions. It does not become a determinate relationship between the human subjects, choices and decisions. It does not also become a determinate relationship expressed in the coinage 'the way'. Decisions in such a mode suspend a one-to-one relationship between acts and choices. Derrida explains the situation in the following way:

> Even when I believe myself to have opted for a decision, I don't know if I have in fact taken a decision, but it is necessary that I

> refer myself to the possibility of this decision and think if *s'il yen a* (the way the things are).[28]

To sum up, the crucial difference between Rortyean pragmatism and Derridean deconstruction lies in their perspective of the nature of reality. For deconstructionists, the possibility of taking decisions stems out of a radical stage of undesirability showing that an already taken decision is supervenient upon the conditions of its possibility, which in themselves are never totally determinable. Pragmatism takes the nature of reality as something arising out of shared needs and produces more of a constructivist account of the human situation and hence conceives any decision as coherent with a set of belief and standards within a particular society. [29]

Notes

1. Richard Rorty, *Essays on Heidegger and others* Cambridge University Press, New York, 1991, p. 92. Henceforth, *EHO*.
2. "Richard Rorty Quotes Derrida", from *MP* in *EHO*, p. 89.
3. *EHO*, p. 87.
4. *EHO*, p. 88.
5. *EHO*, p. 94.
6. *EHO*, p. 97.
7. *EHO*, p. 102.
8. Chantal Moufe, ed. *Deconstruction and Pragmatism*, Routledge, London, 1996, p. 16. Henceforth *DP*.
9. Richard Rorty, *EHO*, p. 117.
10. *EHO*, p. 120.
11. *EHO*, p. 126.
12. *EHO*, p. 126.
13. *EHO*, p. 115.
14. *EHO*, p. 115.
15. *EHO*, p. 131.
16. *EHO*, p. 131.
17. *EHO*, p. 115.
18. *EHO*, p. 136.

19. *EHO*, p. 136.
20. *EHO*, p. 136.
21. *EHO*, p. 115.
22. *EHO*, p. 37.
23. Jacques Derrida, *Writing and Difference*, trans. Alan Bass, Cornell University, Press, 1976, p. 110.
24. *DP*, p. 82.
25. *DP*, p. 82.
26. *DP*, p. 85.
27. *DP*, p. 87.
28. *DP*, p. 87.
29. M.M. Agrawal, *Ethics and Secular Spirituality*, Indian Institute of Advanced Studies, Shimla, 1998, pp. 44-48.

VII

The Postmodern Controversy

*An Evaluation*****

The divergence between Rorty, Derrida and Habermas certainly produces an open-ended play of positions and counter-positions with regard to postmodern and modern understanding of knowledge. Rorty's emphasis on linguistic practices of communities jibes well with Derrida's emphasis on the irreducible structure of difference in any 'postmodern experience'. One may recall the well-known postmodern understanding of experience, formulated in terms of a divided and duplicitous character, which has always already occurred and yet needs to be produced; which becomes an indispensible point of reference, yet it never simply is there. Habermas' position on linguistically mediated social practices as a repository of the normative basis of societies structure language as something in the world and grounds it in actual practices. If postmodernity is characterised by employment of a plural, multiple and self-referential structure of difference in understanding and knowing the world, which Rorty converts into a matter of redescription of the old in a new name, then the question is, can language be thought of as an autonomous and thoroughly free medium that makes all that possible? Taking Habermas as a contrast, one can ask the question, why should language(s) resemble a repository of norms through which humans are able to mutually understand each other? Two basic contradictory theses, therefore, emerge in the divergence between postmodernity and modernity:

(1) Language can operate free of any determinations in order to give a plural description/representation of the world.
(2) Language bears all those norms and rules that govern the actual world in order to be able to affect communication in the world.

A version of (1) is Rorty's ultimate court of appeal in the beliefs of the individual and the community and Derrida's rejection of a causal account of the irreducible structure of difference that language embeds in itself. Rorty and Derrida put together make multiple and plural use of language possible quite in contrast to grammatical, conventional, lexical or morphological rules by prescribing a rather simple and free choice of language. A version of (2) lies in Habermas' discourse ethics in which discourse in language must proceed through observation of universal norms and principles.

The questions that one asks here are: How could use of language be possible without agreement in concepts, definitions and judgements? As Wittgenstein puts it, 'To have agreement in language, we must not only agree on definitions, but there must also be agreement in judgement',[1] which clearly fixes two conditions for any agreement: (1) agreement on definitions and (2) agreement in judgements. So the question is, do Rorty and Derrida follow these conditions of possibility in making their claims about language? Obviously not. The result is Rorty's radical incommensurability thesis which rejects the possibility of minimal agreement on the use of language. For Derrida, it is a thesis of free play that never allows any determination of referents of the signs. Further, Rorty's incommensurability thesis bases itself upon a rejection of a 'mirroring' or 'standing for' relationship between 'signs' and 'world', which is a sequel of the Derridean rejection of 'presence' as well. The problem that crops up because of such radical rejection of all referential bases of language is that a minimal condition of intelligibility is 'lost' in use of language. The danger is two-fold One, what a statement says remains unrecognisable, even what emanates following postmodernist thesis of the play of language remains undecipherable in the very language which produces it. Two, one cannot understand the 'other' without a minimal understanding of what the 'other' is trying to 'mean' in language.

The first danger manifests in Derrida's thesis of difference, which has two moments of operation: one, it locates a chain of difference between signs in which metaphysical opposition are opposed and later transformed into a higher order 'play', and two, the operation in which difference comes to reinscribe the terms in a different order. What Derrida further does not locate is how to recognise difference if there is no agreement on definitions preceding the play of difference. As Derrida places difference as the transcendental condition of the possibility of signification without any determination of a place of the knowing subject, how can one know those conditions of ontological and metaphysical determination of 'concepts' and their 'referents'? Derrida puts forth the claim that there is a fundamental difference between western metaphysics and its non-human outside which produces metaphysics or epistemology as an 'explanation' of the difference without being able to explain it. This is what Derrida considers as being caught within the hermeneutic circle. What Wittgenstein proposes is something dissimilar in its methodology: An agreement on definitions brings about an agreement on judgements; put in an inverse manner, it also includes the possibility of difference through agreement on conventions of use of language. Derrida recognises this when he characterises language as something that eludes the 'play of difference'[2] and questions the possibility of finding out a site or a non-site outside philosophy from where one can question the inside determinations in philosophy.[3] Therefore, a Wittgensteinian intervention in Derrida's notion of difference work as therapy by retaining the criteria of intelligibility in language? Following these, one can agree with Derrida in case one agrees with the definitions of 'presence', 'inside', 'outside', etc., through which his judgement about western philosophy can be understood, which could be an agreement on the meaning of those judgements.

Rorty's thesis on the radical 'incommensurability of paradigm' talks about the possibility of having a plural discourse-relative paradigm, the definitions and judgements of which can be understood only through reference to those paradigms. But the question is, does Wittgenstein's criterion imply a paradigm specific agreement or an agreement in general that makes understanding possible? If it is a paradigm specific agreement on definition and judgement, it would imply that we would *not* differ to be able to understand other paradigms from our own standing in a certain paradigm. The case for having multiple paradigms of reality, for example, science as a paradigmatic expression of culture and language as a paradigmatic expression of social mores, makes a simultaneous possibility of plural understanding of reality, out of which one's choice for a particular paradigm would preclude understanding of other paradigms if there is no common protocol for using language. This means that the radical incommensurability between paradigms would imply 'incommensurability because of unintelligibility'. In other words, Rorty's incommensurability thesis would mean just one way of using language in a certain paradigm that makes other ways un-understandable. One can term it as a closure in just one domain, from where other domains remain invisible and unknowable. To quell such an implication, one must take the position of retaining a general criterion of understanding for even the other paradigms by having a common language in which a minimal agreement on definition and judgement in terms of their understandability will be obtained. Wittgenstein's thesis about language, that to understand a sentence means to understand a language and to understand a language means to be master of a technique,[4] makes it possible to have a general understanding of the terms and concepts of a language, which can be employed variously.

The employment of language for various paradigms can be explained by two basic facts about language: one, defining concepts, etc., in language does not make it possible to share a common paradigm of language by way of mutual agreement on terms, concepts and definitions.

From this position, one can delve a little more into Rorty's incommensurability thesis. Incommensurability has to be understood as a presupposition of understating each such incommensurable paradigm in its own terms and then in terms of the difference of meaning that such paradigms produce. If there is incommunicability between one paradigm and the other, one can either understand each paradigm in its own terms or understand their difference. Therefore, 'incommensurability' may mean total or partial untranslatability as between various language and cultures, but this does not mean incommunicability. The reason is that the incommunicability between language is only an initial phenomenon till one goes into the definitions and concepts of a different language. Only when one has gone into such definitions and concepts can one realise that the difference should be communicable. Incommunicability in a total sense makes the difference unintelligible, hence a minimal criterion of intelligibility needs to be retained for an appreciation of different approaches and frameworks, without which postmodernism as a different philosophical approach would also remain unintelligible.

Now one can extend further this criterion of intelligibility to Habermas' conceptualisation of communication. Habermas' conceptualisation involves a strict norm following behaviour in the use of language. Habermas' thesis that language is the medium of negotiating norms, values and cultural conventions in a rational-procedural mode of following certain universal rules in the use of language is stretching Wittgenstein's criterion too far. The way Habermas formalises norms in order to regulate the use of language presents a more austere and strict criterion for truth and meaning without allowing any possibility of incommensurability. Wittgenstein alters incommensurability by showing that meaning can't be wholly decided, but it can be decided by an agreement on definitions and judgements. Habermas stretches this to evolve universal norms and rules to be followed while using language, which is a different interpretation of Wittgenstien. It reinterprets Wittgenstein with regard to the rules being followed in the use of language that are conceptualised in terms of the actual norms of life that must be followed in conducting a discourse. Wittgenstein does not extend the theory of meaning to construction and participation in discourses; he confines it to the 'form of life' argument or mastering a technique case. Habermas closes upon the form of life argument in terms of certain stable life-world norms, which are preserved in language and practised along with the use of language. Habermas' thesis of communicative action, therefore, turns language into a rule following medium, the rules of which can be justified by appealing to the actual practices of a community. But universalisation of such rules in terms of a common set of universal principles presupposed in any communication is 'intersubjective'[5]. This is a formalisation of Wittgenstein's open-ended rule following thesis of language to use it as a universal criterion of truth and knowledge. The rule following thesis merely retains a minimal criterion of intelligibility without a rule for the interpreter's radical interpretation of a discourse, which should be based on this minimal agreement on definitions.

Rorty's incommensurability thesis, therefore, must base itself upon mutually agreed upon judgement of various discourses, which are different in meaning. This also makes possible a thesis of radical un-translatability as there cannot be a common scheme of translation, because a common scheme of translation would simply mean the possibility of translating concepts in corresponding concepts available in a different language, which may not follow the conventions of the earlier language. But the question arises, does 'radical untranslatability' imply 'incommunicability'? Wittgenstein's answer to this question comes from his notion of 'family resemblance', which is 'a complicated network of similarities overlapping and criss-crossing'[6] between radically incommensurable discourses and their homologues or analogues with whom they bear some 'family resemblance'. Such 'family resemblance' again retains a seminal possibility of similarity out of total dissimilar discourses, which in themselves remain dissimilar while they resemble something in common through their similarities with some other discourses. For example, similarity between the Wittgensteinian 'use theory of meaning' and Habermas' communicative action in terms of 'rule following' and ultimate appeal to 'conventions' could be a 'criss-cross', but they remain incommensurable in terms of Habermas' translation of rule following in language as an equivalent case of following a set of universal rules by various human individuals engaged in a discourse. While Wittgenstein's position resembles Habermas' and vice versa, they remain incommensurable; As in Wittgenstein, there are no universal rules to be followed in the use of language, while in Habermas, there are universal rules that must be followed in the use of language. They are incommensurable in their theory of meaning, while they are communicable as both theories maintain a general agreement on the use of terms and concepts despite their disagreement on definitions and judgements. Such disagreement gives rise to 'incommensurability', but it does not make it impossible to understand each other's positions. Therefore, Rorty's thesis of incommensurability entailing 'incommunicability' has to be rejected following the Wittgensteinian criterion of 'agreement'. Derrida's thesis of an irreducible structure of difference implying a play of meaning can only be understood in terms of a prior understanding of difference in terms of the meanings agreed upon, as Derrida explains it.

Reapprising the Status of Philosophy

Rorty's thesis on the end of philosophy based upon a critique of foundationalism further problematises the notion of philosophy. Postmodernism's general rejection of foundationalism and the principle of reason implies a radical rejection of philosophy in general and its replacement with the possibility of free play of language. But the question that should be asked here is, what kind of free play postmodernism contends, is it absolute or confined within some discourse and conceptual framework? Rorty's rejection of foundationalism in the form of a world totally lost except to be found in language implies the causal power of the world to produce representations. But this counter-thesis to 'representationalism' itself takes a metaphysical form as representations are caused by a world already captured in language. This is a strange metaphysical circle in which the world remains as a representation, while simultaneously causes 'representations'. Is it then that 'representations' cause 'representation' without any correlates in the world? Rorty obviously gives a picture of correlation through a pragmatic invocation of 'social practice', which gives rise to the causality between world and language, thereby meaning that social practices enforces a kind of 'world-language' relationship which does not allow the world as a knowable unless it is represented within language. If that be so, the contingency of social practices would never let us move out of this hermeneutic circle of the 'social practice-world-language' chain and vice versa, thereby closing upon us a sense of the irreducibility of this relationship. In a reverse way, this would mean that meanings in language are reducible to this circle. Anti-foundationalism of this nature gives a criterion of truth in terms of 'success' of particular social practices in a 'community', which is a matter of sharing a 'common interpretation'. Does not this anti-foundationalism give rise to an extreme form of metaphysical representationalism, which removes all worldly practices and language that are already there without being caused by anything? Therefore, Rorty had to give an anti-anti-foundational definition of cause in terms of 'brute facts', which is something 'out there', an example of eating humble pie in which 'most things in space and time are the effects of cause which do not include human mental states'? Rorty elucidates the notion of the world as a causal force which precedes the world as we know it and, therefore, anchors our mental representations in terms of a causal role of the world represented as a 'brute force' in us. This anti-anti-foundationalism of Rorty is just a rejection of a claim of the veracity or verifications of representation generally advocated in realism, but it only provides a different causal picture of reality. Therefore, the postmodernist position of situating everything within the text or representation does not give it a determinate 'closure', rather it is open to contexts in general. Derrida's famous dictum that 'there is nothing outside the text' simultaneously presumes the world within the text as well as rejects the 'world' outside the text. This formulation is 'ambivalent' the way Rorty is also 'ambivalent' in giving us a causal picture of the world because it turns out to be a world standing outside. Similarly, the case of free play in language can only generate and problematise the world by way of producing different descriptions of it in various discourses, cultures and languages without giving a specific criterion of meaning and truth about it.

Habermas' neutralisation of the world in terms of those rules that govern our relationship with the world and the preservation of those rules within language as a guarantee for 'communicability' further reifies the world-language relationship in some formal descriptive categories. This makes 'communication' an effect of this relationship. Paradoxically enough, Habermas reduces the human subject through such linguistically mediated communication, which makes his thesis vulnerable to subjective free play, which, in his account, language cannot accommodate. So, the question comes back, what do we communicate? Is it a set of rules that is shared intersubjectively or those conditions of possibility to communication that act as transcendental presuppositions of communication?

Communication Only Divides

To find an answer to this question of communication, which neither postmodernists nor modernists seem to give in clear terms, one should take a step beyond this divide between world and language and chart out an alternative understanding of communication. The common lesson that can be drawn from the postmodernist and modernist positions is that 'communication only divides': It says what it says and it does say what it does not say. It differentiates the two and connects them with a boundary that separates the two sides of what is communicated and what is not. No communication can take place beyond what it says and what it does not say, that is to an unmarked space. Further, no backward bending from what it says or what it does not say is possible to lead us to something primordial. If these limits are accepted, then communication acts like a repetitive reproduction of such limits.

Therefore, the world cannot appear just as a piece of information, for it could be a choice from among many different possibilities by human subjects. The world is only that which endures the 'limits' and the boundary between what is said and what is not said, which further makes impossible any regress from this distinction. Communication only reproduces these distinctions by reference to entries in the world in such a manner that we exercise regularity in the act of referring.

Now, the question is how to thematise this 'difference' and 'reference' within communication itself. Difference must be thematised as a unity between communication and non-communication, that is within communication, the world is given only as a paradox. The act of communication severs its unity and affirms its unity implicitly by severing it. It negates this unity by reconstructing it at the level of representation. 'Implicitly' is only to indicate that an observer can see and describe things in this way. Statements about existence and negations belong to signifiers of linguistically constituted communication, but this can only take place on this side of the boundary that is being renewed by such use, but not transgressed by it. This is what brings forth Wittgenstein's notion of 'rule following' and 'agreement'.

In society which includes all possible communications, such a closure bifurcates the world into two: Either a meaning is communicated or it is not. The communicated meaning and the un-communicated one are known only through a prior division of the world, which is explicitly communicated in it. Any alternative to something that is communicated is communicated within the implicit sense of being a communication, a division of the world. Any third possibility of an instance of communication not communicating anything could be ruled out. But does this allow us to distinguish a case of silence? Within communication, silence could be marked by an observer as a case of 'failure' or as a case of withdrawal of the distinction between what is communicated and what is not communicated. This also becomes a problem of distinction leading to a distinction of distinctions: (1) distinction between communicable and not communicable and (2) distinction between what is communicated and what is not communicated. What is communicated can be incommunicable if it maintains a distinction that is transgressed in the same act of communication and what is not communicated could become communicable if what it does not say is distinguishable in what it says. Therefore, one should draw a distinction between the problem of reference and problem of communication in terms of the boundary between what is said and what is not said in it. This can be best understood in Derrida's language of deconstruction:

> Violently inscribing within the text that which attempts to govern it from outside, I try to respect as vigorously possible the internal, regulated play of philosophemes by making them slide (...) to the point of their non-pertinence, their exhaustion, their closure.[8]

So what comes back is the notion of a certain 'closure', borders of a language frame which assumes both conditional and un-conditional character. This makes possible both thinking through reason and through unreason, which becomes a task of interpretation. Only interpretation can provide 'good reasons' or justifications for both these kinds of possibilities.

This also comes close to Derrida's notion of deferral of meaning from signifier to signifier in the process of communication. The meaning of an utterance, for Derrida, is constituted by the interpretation given to it by an addressee and the addressee is perpetually 'absent' in the utterance. The addressee is reconstituted as another absentee once somebody interprets the utterance. It is something like saying that what an utterance gives is not redeemable from a defined context of life, but merely divides the world into two between an absent addressee and its interpretations. While for Habermas, the addressees are constituted by linguistic mediation at a focal point where an utterance and its interpretation criss-cross, a point which is argumentatively redeemable following the norm of communication. But the 'message' and the world cannot be removed in argumentatively redeemable rules of communication because that will assume a set relationship between communication and the world without various 'language games' which keep open the relationship between communication and the world.

An Evaluation

The problem in comparing Richard Rorty, Jacques Derrida and Jurgen Habermas lies in their radical divergence in different theoretical routes. Rorty suggests an open-ended possibility of a practice that does not divide the world into dual domains, but constitutes a holistic world comprising human subjects and the various ways in which they can make the world, while Derrida envisages constant play of oppositions without any final closure. These two positions of Rorty and Derrida posit that the world, as a disclosure within human language, consists of double moves, 'calling an other and repeating the same' simultaneously. This again produces a theory of the world, and a theory purports a singular comprehension by neutralising the subject. The question that we ask here is, does comparison neutralise the world into a totality of fixed meaning? Or does comparison open up a game of interpretation?

Retaining our basic probe into the nature of knowledge, we have already explored some possibilities. For Rorty, the postmodern episteme gives rise to a view of the world, culturally united in certain forms of practices that overrule dichotomies in theories and also constituting an edifying view of the world in which conversation rules life. The possibilities of a culturally unified view of the world exhibiting pluralities of cultural life displace the constraints that tie life to certain forms of metaphysical and epistemological assumptions. For Derrida, the postmodern possibility is that of certain forms of practices and most significantly, deconstructive practices of play that lead to a defiance of conceptual, metaphysical and ideological closure. For both of them, the most empowering concept is the possibility of an open-ended interaction in language, which brings in a notion of emancipated human subjects, emancipated from the closures of modernity.

For Habermas, the possibilities of critique of knowledge stem out of the social crisis and re-orientation of social life. This is possible only by answering the necessity of praxis in an increasingly fragmented, colonised and instrumentalised social world, growing out of systematic intervention. This provides a context of knowledge-constructive interest as well as a reconstructive possibility of universalisable, common and pragmatic frames of knowledge. Such reconstructive possibilities are finally appropriated in the dialogic and inter-subjective sphere of norms available in human discourse to emerge into a communicative praxis. There are basically two moves within such reconstruction of knowledge: one, cognitively justified, morally right and aesthetically good founding of human knowledge, and two, enframing it without a universalisable normative theory and thereby leaving no room for interrogating its authenticity. Such a take of knowledge in an all-comprehensive manner rests upon the social world that incorporates and structures the normative aspects of society within itself. It is a configuration that links up the needs of various spheres of life. Within such a pragmatic construction of knowledge, which is basically a reproduction of the norm for a systematically organised modern social world, human thought, feelings and necessities are streamlined towards some resolutions within the social world. Possibilities like misery, frustration, unfulfilment, which are human predicaments, get dissolved within such paradigmatic forms of knowledge. These get dissolved by systematic and knowledge-constructive interests that churn them in the integrated spheres of life under modernity. It can be summed up that Habermas leaves no rooms for 'derivations' of a human kind, which definitely include creative impulses stretching through a herd of queer passions (love, hate, crime, etc.) as marks of idiosyncrasies. The Habermasian paradigm of knowledge finishes off the epistemic possibility of expression of such human predicaments.

What emerges is a choice between disclosure of the world and construction of a social world as it emerges in Rorty and Derrida on the one hand, and Habermas on the other. The possible disclosure of the world in the edification within language is a postmodern characteristic, while agreement upon rules and norms of society as immanent is modern in nature. The two stand as mutually incommensurable prospects. One can further distinguish these two possibilities by way of noting that postmodern possibilities emerge from an exotic use of language, while modern emerges from the structuring of reality in language. Modern aims at making the immanent visible from within language, while postmodern aims at bringing out what is not immanent within language, if immanent is constituted by the normative structures of society. Modern creates this problem or dichotomy between norms and meaning by way of immanent and not immanent, an inside and an outside, which has been critiqued in Rorty and Derrida. Postmodern radically displaces one side of the dichotomy into the 'other' and attempts at closing the difference. Further language in its own way helps the subject to negotiate this difference. Given that under Modern, the conception of immanent lies within language, what is not immanent also arises within language and language contains this difference within. Modern contains this difference through the criteria of practice. It is a two-fold criterion; whether we bother about such a difference or not, it becomes a linguistic practice in order to negotiate with social practices. Rorty denies a practice of differentiation between language and social practice within language itself. The interior of differentiation and hierarchisation with which we operate in practice, within modernity, gets modified within our linguistic practice. Therefore, postmodernism shelves the moral and metaphysical criterion that induces a distinction between values and facts in our linguistic practice as such a distinction reinforces the differences within practice. Rather, it contends that linguistic practice, in its own way does not admit this criterion of distinction. As linguistic practice does not go by such criterion of distinction as is available in social practice, it either affects dissolution of such distinctions in social practice or retains it. In Modern, the distinction of norms and facts is maintained in language. Postmodern, does not admit such a distinction.

Postmodernism, therefore, does not adopt a theory of knowledge, but begins from a repudiation of theoretical distinctions and exercises like modern criteria of reference, truth and knowledge,. It explores the possibility of repudiation of these distinctions of modern epistemology, but takes it as it is, without maintaining the practice of differentiation and hierarchisation. Derrida's concept of writing further relegates this world of modernity into concept-metaphors that restructure its entangled relationship with the world and assumes synonymity or analogy with other concepts.

Philosophy as a source of writing, as Rorty describes it following Derrida, gives a notion of writing in signifying that genre which, as a law, both holds and expels its member. Philosophy, for postmodernism, as a genre, holds an 'excess', an exterior that exceeds its closure of concepts:

1. Rorty holds that social practice produces beliefs about right and wrong about the world. Beliefs of this kind are held in concepts in language.
2. Derrida brings out the concept-metaphors as signifiers in the play of oppositions that simultaneously contextualises and problematises language.
3. Habermas brings out a stable normative basis of social life organised into a coherent whole which takes precedence over linguistic practices and enacts a foundational criterion of determination of meaning.
4. The way Rorty presents his whole idea of belief as a source of meaning and knowledge distantiates his theory from Derrida's notion of deconstruction, which allegedly circumvents belief within culture. This premonition of self-subversive play of deconstruction, according to Rorty, produces a flux that disrupts the social process of weaving and reweaving beliefs.
5. Derrida's deconstruction questions supposedly legitimate, justified and valid moral norms by exposing their repressive interior, by exposing how suppress difference and otherness. This aspect of deconstruction radically affects the domain of communication by foregrounding the deconstructive tenet that iterability of the speech-act determines its context and not the other way round. Iterability here means the contextualisation of already given meaning in speech-acts and contextualising those speech acts in contrast to the linear 'meaning-context' relationship assumed in the speech-act.
6. Habermas' critique of Rorty for abandonment of the criterion of knowledge and conflation of language with ontology re-iterates the modernist critique of

postmodernisation. But Rorty refutes such charges by a notion of creativity in the poetic use of language that also presents the possibility of establishing social justice in order to meet our common goals. What we require is only a linguistic practice that redescribes the affairs of the world in coherence with our belief of good.

7. Habermas' critique of Derrida for being monotheistic and bringing the world under the unitary notion of being is already thwarted in Derrida's deconstruction of the notion of being in a negative theology that conceptualises logos or being as permanently absent. Such a primordial absence empties out the unitary metaphysical determination of being and forces us to accept a notion of being as it is juxtaposed against the non-identity of beings.

To sum up, postmodernism prioritises language as the primary source of reason and cognition, which is brought out in both Rorty and Derrida's work. For Habermas, however, language is constituted by the human subject and such a constitution is inter-subjective in nature, which represents a linguistic version of the modern theory of knowledge.

Notes

1. Ludwig Wittgenstein, *Philosophical Investigations*, Macmillan, New York, 1971, No. 242. Henceforth *PI*.
2. Jacques Derrida, *MP*, p. 11.
3. Jacques Derrida, *P*. p. 107.
4. *PI*, no. 199.
5. Habermas does not attach any significance to cultural difference or unknowability of 'core' aspects of other cultures. He reduces such differences under the universalisability of some common norms of human communication.
6. Ludwig Wittgenstein, *PI*, pp. 66, 67.
7. Richard Rorty, *ORT*, pp. 81-101, 84, 166, and *CIS*, p. 5.
8. Jacques Derrida, *P*, p. 6.

Bibliography

Agrawal, Murari M., *Ethics and Secular Spirituality*, Indian Institute of Advanced Studies, Shimla, 1998.

Antony, Louise, "Quine as Feminist: The Radical Import of Naturalized Epistemology" in Lousie M. Antony and Charlotte Witt. A *Mind of One's Own: Feminist Essays on Reason and Objectivity*, Westview, Boulder: Colorado, 1993.

Benhabib, Seyla, "Autonomy, Modernity and Community: Communication and Critical Theory in Dialogue" in *Zwischenbetrachtungen im Prozess der Aufklarung*, ed. Axel Honneth Sukhramo, Frankfurt, 1988.

— *Situating the Self*, Routledge, New York, 1992.

Bernstein, Richard, *Habermas and Modernity*, MIT Press, Cambridge, 1985.

Bilgrami, Akeel, *Belief and Meaning*, Blackwell, Oxford, 1992.

Chalmers, David, *The Conscious Mind: In Search of a Fundamental Principle*, Oxford University Press, New York, 1996.

Coward, Harold and Foshay, T. (eds.), *Derrida and Negative Theology*, SUNY Press, Albany, 1992.

Davidson, Donald, "Nice Derangement of Epitaph" in. *Truth and Interpretation*, ed. Ernest Lepore, Blackwell, Oxford, 1986, pp. 433-46.

Derrida, Jacques, *Speech and Phenomena and Other Essays on Husserl's Theory of Signs*, trans. David Allison, Northwestern University Press, Evanston, 1973.

— *L' Archeologie du frivole*, Lire Condilla, Denoël/Gonthier, Paris, 1976.

— *Of Grammatology*, trans. Gayatri Chakraborty Spivak, John Hopkins University Press, Baltimore, 1976.

— *Writing and Difference*, trans. Alan Bass, University. of Chicago Press, Chicago, 1978.

— *Spurs: Nietzsche's Styles*, trans. Barbara Harlow, University of Chicago Press, 1978.

— "Living on/Border Lines", trans. James Hulbert, in *Deconstruction and Criticism*, Harold Bloom et al., Continuum, New York, 1979.

— *Dissemination*, trans. Barbara Johnson, University of Chicago Press, Chicago, 1981.

— *Positions*, trans. Alan Bass, University of Chicago Press, Chicago, 1981.

— *Margins of Philosophy*, trans. Alan Bass, University of Chicago Press, Chicago, 1982.

— "Of An Apocalyptic Tone Recently Adopted in Philosophy", trans John P. Leavey Jr, *Semeia*, 23, 1982.

— "The Principle of Reason: The University in the Eyes of its Pupils", *Diacritics*, Fall 1983, pp. 3-20.

— *Parages*, Galilee, Paris, 1986.

— *Glas*, trans. John P. Leavey Jr, University of Nebraska Press, Lincoln, 1983.

— *Limited Inc. a,b,c.*, trans. Samuel Weber, Northwestern University Press, Evanston, 1988.

— *Reading de Man Reading*, ed. Lindsay Waters and Wlad Godzich, University of Minnesota Press, Minneapolis, 1989.

— "How to Avoid Speaking" in *Language of The Unsayable*, eds. S. Budick and W. Iser, Columbia University Press, New York, 1989, pp. 3-70.

— *The Other Heading: Reflections on Today's Europe* trans. P.A. Brault et al., Indiana University Press, Bloomington, 1992.

— *Raising the Tone of Philosophy: Late Essays by Immanuel Kant, Transformative Critique by Jacques Derrida*, ed. Peter Fenves, John Hopkins University Press, Baltimore, 1993.

— *Word Traces: Readings of Paul Celan*, ed. A. Fioretes, John Hopkins University Press, Baltimore 1994.

— *Spectres of Marx*, trans. Peggy Kamuf, Routledge, New York, 1994.

— *Points ... Interviews 1974-97*, ed. Elisabeth Weber, trans. Peggy Kamuf et al., Stanford University Press, Stanford, 1995.

— "Archive Fever: A Freudian Impression", trans. Eric Perenowitz, *Diacritics*, 25 (1995), pp. 9-63.

Farrell, Frank B., *Subjectivity, Realism and Postmodernism: The Recovery of the World in Recent Philosophy*, Cambridge University Pres, Cambridge, 1994.

Geras, Norman, Solidarity in the Conversation *of Human Kind: The Ungroundable Liberalism of Richard Rorty*, Verso, London, 1995.

Habermas, Jurgen, "Towards a Theory of Communicative Competence" in *Recent Sociology*, 2(1970), ed. H.P. Dreitzel, Macmillan.

— *Knowledge and Human Interest*, trans. Jeremy I. Shapiro, Beacon Press, Boston, 1971.

— "A Reply to My Critics" in *Habermas: Critical Debates*, eds. B. Thompson and D. Held, Macmillan, London, 1982.

— *Philosophical Discourse of Modernity*, trans. T. McCarthy, Polity Press, Cambridge, 1985.

— *Theory of Communicative Action*, Vol. I & II, trans. Thomas McCarthy, Polity Press, Cambridge, 1987.

— *Moral Consciousness and Communicative Action*, trans. C. Lenhart and S. W., Nicholson. MIT Press, Cambridge, Massachusetts, 1990.

— "Justice and Solidarity: On the Discussion Concerning State - 6" in *The Philosophical Forum*, XXI: 1-2, pp. 32-51.

— *Postmetaphysical Thinking*, trans. W.M. Hohengarten, Cambridge, Massachusetts, 1992.

— "Volkssoouveranital als ver fahren" in *Faklizitat and Geltung*, Frankfurt am Main, 1992.

— *Justification and Application*, trans. Ciaran Cronia, Polity Press, Cambridge, 1993.

— *Between Facts and Norms: Contributions to a Discourse Theory of Law and Democracy*, trans. W. Rehg, Polity Press, Cambridge, 1995.

Hall, David L., *Richard Rorty: Prophet and Poet of New Pragmatism*, SUNY, Anbany, 1994.

Harlow, Barbara, "A Discussion with Jacques Derrida", *Writing Instructor*, Vol. 9 No. 1-2, 1989.

Heidegger, Martin, *The End of Philosophy*, Harper and Row, New York, 1973.

Hume, David, *An Enquiry Concerning Human Understanding*, ed. Eric Steinberg, 2nd ed., Hackett Publishing, Company, Indianapolis, 1993.

Husserl, Edmund, *Ideas*, Vol. I, trans. W. Boyce Gibson, Collier Books, New York, 1962.

Man, Paul de, "Phenomenality and Materiality in Kant" in *Hermeneutics: Questions and Prospects*, eds. Gary Shapiro and Alan Sica, University, of Massachusetts Press, Amherst, 1984.

McCarthy', Thomas: "Ironist Theory as a Vocation: A Response to Rorty's Reply", *Critical Inquiry*, 16 (1990).

MeCumber, John, "Reconnecting Rorty: The Situation of Discourse in Richard Rorty's Contingency, Irony and Solidarity", *Diacritics*, 20 (1990), pp. 2-19.

Mouffe, Chantal et al. (ed.) *Deconstruction and Pragmatism*, Routledge, London, 1996.

O'Neill, Onora, *Constructions of Reasons: Exploration of Kant's Practical Philosophy*, Cambridge University Press, Cambridge, 1989.

Rorty, Richard, *Philosophy and the Mirror of Nature*, Basil Blackwell, 1980.

— *Consequences of Pragmatism*, University of Minnesota Press, Minneapolis, 1982.

— *Contingency, Irony and Solidarity*, Cambridge University Press, Cambridge. 1989.

— *Objectivity, Relativism and Truth: Philosophical Papers*, Vol. I, Cambridge University Press, Cambridge, 1991.

— *Essays on Heidegger and Others: Philosophical Paper*, Vol, II, Cambridge University Press, 1991.

— "Is Truth A Goal of Inquiry? Right vs. Davidson", *The Philosophical Quarterly*, Vol. 45.3, No. 180, 1995.

— "Against Unity" in *Wilson Review*, October 1998.

Schwyzer, Hubert, "Subjectivity in Descartes and Kant", *The Philosophical Quarterly*, Vol. 47, no. 188, 1997.

Steinhoff, Uwe, "Truth Vs. Rorty", *The Philosophical Quarterly*, Vol. 47, No. 188, 1997.

Stroud, Barry, "Kantian Argument, Conceptual Capacities and Invulnerability" in ed. Paolo Parrini, *Kant and Contemporary Epistemology*, Kluwer, Dordrecht, 1994, pp. 231-51.

Wittgenstein, Ludwig, *Philosophical Investigations*, Macmillan, New York, 1971.

Wreen, Michael, "Yes, Virginia, There is a Santa Claus", *Informal Logic*, I 1987, pp. 34-39.

Index